THE CHANNEL I

To experience the Channel Island

"How can places that should be s
that will pop into the mind of anyc
for the first time. While it is easy to package Jersey, Guernsey, Alderney, Sark and Herm under all kinds of umbrellas, this new 110-mile, island-hopping walking route completely dispels the notion that any of the five islands are similar to their neighbours. In fact the further you walk the more you will see how each island asserts its own unique charm and personality. From the timeless charm of Herm's Shell Beach to Alderney's heaving sea bird colonies and Sark, with its horse and tractor bus transport system, each of the islands has its own character.

This wonderful walking route provides an ideal way to explore the stunningly diverse coastlines of Jersey and Guernsey as well as the three smaller islands. When even the largest island, Jersey, can be circumnavigated on foot in four days, all five destinations fit easily into the 'short break' category. And with a well-planned itinerary it is entirely feasible to walk the whole set in under a fortnight.

But why rush? After spending one holiday break walking around one of the bigger islands, why not take in a selection of the smaller ones on your next visit? Or perhaps you would prefer to do it the other way, starting with an adventure by boat to discover the delights of Herm and Sark before moving onto Guernsey, Jersey and Alderney?

Putting the pleasures of walking these dramatic and ever changing coastlines to one side, the compact nature of the islands means that the comforts of a friendly café, a welcoming pub or a lovely little restaurant are never far away. On the bigger islands the Channel Island Way is divided into easily manageable sections with toilets, cafés and bus stops located conveniently at the recommended start and finish points.

The beauty of the Channel Island Way, apart from the breathtaking scenery of our lovely coastlines, is that there is no set rulebook to say how much ground you should cover in any one visit or on any one day. With this guide we have provided you with the perfect companion to help you choose and the rest is up to you.

Finally, please be aware that the terrain of some of the walks (mostly along Jersey's north coast and Guernsey's south coast) means there are a lot of steps, which could be hard on the knees!

Coast MEDIA Tel: 01481 735450
www.coastmediaci.com

Words: Arthur Lamy. **Photography:** Chris George Photography, Coast Media Limited.

COVER PICTURE: Pathway alongside Fishermans Beach, Herm.
Tel: 01481 735461 www.chrisgeorgephotography.net

Section 1 - **JERSEY**

The Around Island Walk

However you plan to experience Jersey's diverse and dynamic coastline, whether you propose to walk the entire 48 miles or just sample a few miles here and there, you will discover a new panorama around every corner. No matter where you walk, or how far, Jersey's coastline will always reward the curious, and create memories that last forever.

Although the coast is not short of places to stop for refreshment, it is wise to carry water and a snack. A mobile phone is also a good idea, but remember that you might not always get a signal on our north coast. A bus timetable and a tide table can be very useful too. Where there is no pavement it is safest to walk on the right hand side of the road in single file. Finally, Jersey has one of the largest and fastest ranges of tide in the world, so make sure that you can cross a beach without becoming trapped by the incoming tide.

Some useful phone numbers

The dialling code for Jersey is 01534.

Jersey Tourism	Telephone: 448877
Connex Buses	Telephone: 877772
Weather Forecast	Telephone: 0900 6650011
Ambulance	Telephone: 624700
Fire	Telephone: 633506
Police	Telephone: 612612
Sea Rescue	Telephone: 885588

In an emergency dial 112 or 999

La Rocco Tower, St Ouen's Bay

Mont Orgueil Castle, Gorey

Using this guide

The distances between these suggested stops vary, so approximate milages have been given to help plan your walk. All 16 points are accessible by bus, but please check the timetable, and most have car parking and toilet facilities. There are usually cafés, public houses or restaurants open nearby but, again, check before setting out.

Suggested stops

1 ELIZABETH QUAY FERRY TERMINAL
Car Parking, Public Toilets, Café, Restaurant, Bus Route 19

2 LA ROCQUE HARBOUR
Car Parking, Public Toilets, Bus Route 1

3 GOREY VILLAGE
Car Parking, Public Toilets, Café, Restaurants, Bus Route 1,1b

4 ST CATHERINE'S BREAKWATER
Car Parking, Public Toilets, Café, Bus Route 1b

5 ROZEL BAY*
Public Toilets, Cafés, Restaurants, Pub, Bus Route 3

6 BONNE NUIT*
Public Toilets, Café, Bus Route 4

7 DEVIL'S HOLE
Car Parking, Pub, Bus Route 27

8 GREVE DE LECQ
Car Parking, Public Toilets, Café, Restaurant, Pubs, Bus Route 9

9 PLEMONT
Car Parking, Public Toilets, Café, Bus Route 8

10 L'ETACQ
Car Parking, Bus Route 12a

11 THE WATERSPLASH
Car Parking, Café, Bus Route 12a

12 LA PULENTE
Car Parking, Public Toilets, Restaurants, Bus Route 12a

13 LA CORBIERE
Car Parking, Public Toilets, Restaurant, Bus Route 12

14 ST BRELADE'S BAY
Car Parking, Public Toilets, Cafés, Restaurant, Pubs, Bus Route 12

15 OLD PORTELET INN
Car Parking, Restaurant, Pub, Bus Route 12

16 ST AUBIN'S VILLAGE
Car Parking, Public Toilets, Cafés, Restaurants, Pubs, Bus Route 12,12a,15

* Limited Car Parking

ELIZABETH QUAY FERRY TERMINAL

Distance:
5 Miles

Bus Number:
19

Toilets:
Yes

Car Parking:
Yes

Food:
Café, Restaurant

Looking towards Fort Regent from Old Harbour

ELIZABETH QUAY FERRY TERMINAL

Leave the Ferry Terminal and follow the road to the left as it heads towards the town of St Helier. Pass two double-gabled warehouses on the right, then take the first right to emerge on a pier bordered by white railings.

Bearing left, walk over to the railings adjacent to the harbour and continue beside them towards the top of the pier. At the top, turn right to follow the walkway passing the Liberation Statue on the left and the Steam Clock on the right.

1. The Steam Clock

Conceived by the artist Gordon Young and manufactured by Smith of Derby, the clock was commissioned in 1997 and acts as a focal point on the far side of the dual carriageway. It is an authentic full size replica of a paddle steamer and is named Ariadne, after one of the first steam powered boats to visit Jersey in the early part of the 19th century. The coming of steam, which offered the visitor a regular and reliable service, saw the birth of a fledgling tourism industry. However, the arrival of steam power and steel ships did herald the decline of Jersey's prosperous shipbuilding trade. The benches which we shall pass presently, the work of Russell Coleman, serve as a memorial to those ships and the yards that built them.

Where the walkway ends, cross straight over to carry on between the 'ship' benches and the railings bordering the harbour. When we reach the end of the railings, tide permitting, turn right to cross the small harbour. Once out of the harbour, walk along a short stretch of pavement before dropping into another small harbour. Climb the steps and turn left immediately to cross to a flight of steps directly across the road.

At the top of the steps turn right. When the pavement ends, cross diagonally to descend to another short flight of steps. Climb the steps and follow the pavement as it rises.

Just before a patch of grass, surrounded by a small hedge, bear to the right to descend between a tall granite wall and the power station on the right. When the slope flattens, bear left to continue along the old promenade as it skirts the beach at Havre des Pas. Walk on, crossing a slipway and passing hotels and restaurants until emerging beside the main road. Here, turn right to pass the Bathing Pool, a large building joined to the land by a jetty.

2. The Bathing Pool

In the early 1890s, proposals were made for a ladies' bathing pool at Havre des Pas. At that time gentlemen had their own rudimentary sea bathing facility at La Collette, close to the start of the promenade. After several meetings, it was decided that responsibility for this should fall to the Jersey Swimming Club. The club agreed to this; in 1893 it became incorporated and the lease of the foreshore at Havre des Pas was granted to the club by Queen Victoria. To raise the money, the club issued £5 debenture bonds, bearing 2.5% interest.

By the turn of the century the ongoing plans for a separate men's pool had been shelved. Men were now allowed to use the women's pool, providing that they paid 7/6d (37p) in addition to their annual subscription. Needless to say, this was not allowed in the company of ladies. By 1904 mixed bathing had at last been introduced, but only between the hours of 9 and 10.30 in the morning!

Pass the Bathing Pool and the ornate Victorian facades of the hotels and houses, until we reach a junction, where we turn right towards a squat granite building beside a slipway. Follow the pavement, passing the slipway and the granite building on your right. In the last few yards we have left St Helier and are now in the narrow strip of St Saviour that boasts a coastline and within minutes we will be in St Clement.

Today, St Clement is a very highly populated parish and our view of the sea will be occasionally interrupted by buildings. We pass a filling station on the left and soon reach a slipway which heralds another stretch of beachside walking. This section of coastline is naturally defended by a barrier of treacherous rocks and therefore wartime defences are fairly rare. One of the few German defences in the area borders this slipway. This particular bunker has become a public toilet, which must make it one of the safest places to 'spend a penny' in the island!

The dangers of the surrounding reefs are further endorsed by the lighthouse on the sea wall ahead.

One cluster of rocks is well known; La Sambue is one of the largest and it can be recognised by a taller outcrop at each end, rather like a pair of stunted horns.

La Sambue

On 13th September 1949 the 10 ton cutter the Maurice Georges was homeward bound from St Malo. She had four people on board and had run out of fuel just off the Demi des Pas beacon. With bad visibility and a strong tide running, the captain was forced to drop anchor. This held for some time but finally broke, leaving the craft at the mercy of the surrounding rocks.

While this was happening, another boat was also low on fuel, but it too was nearly home. This was the Jersey relief lifeboat, the Hearts of Oak, with coxswain Tommy King at the helm. The lifeboat was returning from nine hours at sea, spent searching fruitlessly for the survivors of a French military plane that had ditched in the sea, 20 miles south east of the island. It was around midnight when the Hearts of Oak received the call that an SOS signal had been seen coming from rocks near La Sambue.

On hearing this, the lifeboat immediately turned about and made its way out into the open sea again. Once close to the Maurice Georges, coxswain King could see how difficult the rescue would be. The boat was surrounded on all sides by rocks and, with an ebbing tide, the situation was getting worse by the minute.

Undeterred, the lifeboat drew closer. Seeing that going in close to pick up the crew would be impossible, coxswain King decided to throw a line between the boats and tow the Maurice Georges clear. Within 15 minutes both boats were clear of the reefs and in open water.

For this act of gallantry coxswain Tommy King received the RNLI Gold Medal, while each of the lifeboat men received a RNLI Bronze Medal. The citation read: 'For this most gallant and resolute service carried out against the gravest perils by a crew already weary from a long and heavy strain'.

The pavement dips and rises as it passes La Mare slipway. Once again we lose sight of the sea as we pass a shop and a tiny Methodist chapel on the left. Avoid a turning on the right that goes to the sea at Green Island. Within 100 yards we arrive at a rather grand, gated entrance which guards a rocky outcrop in the middle of the drive. This is the Rocqueberg, or Witches' Rock.

3. The Rocqueberg

Ths huge, solitary rock stands rather eerily in a grove of trees, and has had long associations with witchcraft. As anyone

Seymour Tower, La Rocque

who has climbed the rock will testify, the impression of a cloven hoof can be clearly seen on its surface. With such a satanic endorsement, it comes as no surprise that the rock was considered a favourite meeting place for a coven of witches.

One tale that comes from the legend describes how fishermen, passing the promontory on which the Rocqueberg stands, would be obliged to pay the witches a toll in the form of the 13th fish from their catch. Failure to do this would result in the witches raising up a horrific storm in which the unfortunate fisherman would perish. In fact, it was known that many who had refused to pay the toll soon met with a watery grave.

This, however, was not the case for one young man. As he returned home he passed close to the promontory, where the witches could be seen busily engaged in their disgusting work. Drawing nearer, he reached down into the boat to pick up his 13th fish, a giant five armed starfish. Cutting off an arm with his knife, he threw the starfish into the middle of the coven, shouting: "The cross is my passport". The starfish landed among the witches in the shape of the cross. Since then, no witches have been seen at the Rocqueberg.

Walk on until the pavement ends, then cross over to continue eastwards on the far pavement. On reaching a small war memorial, slightly set back, in front of St Clement's Parish Hall, cross over again to a patch of grass that borders the beach. Carry on in the direction of the Jersey round tower, Le Hocq Tower, leaving the green by the gap in the roadside wall. Bear right to follow the main road as it climbs gently to the left. When the pavement ends, walk on the roadside for a short distance.

After the slipway, we regain the pavement but lose our sea view for a mile or so. The styles and ancestry of the houses on both sides of the road vary immensely, but two small cottages, set next to each other, on the other side of the road are worth more than a cursory glance.

4. Louvain and Summerleigh

Now owned by the National Trust for Jersey, these two small cottages are beautiful examples of 19th century architecture. Both are of granite with brick edging to the door and windows. Built in the early part of the century, Louvain has a lintel over the front door dated 1835. Very little has changed at all to these properties, although Louvain has had its original pan tile roof replaced with slates.

The road meanders, rises and falls, as we approach Jersey's south-east corner at La Rocque Harbour. As we get nearer, look out for a rectangular granite parish boundary stone beside the pavement. These stones traditionally have the names of each constable, or head of the parish, on them. A close inspection of this one will reveal the date: 1909, CJ Pepin as constable of Grouville and EL Mourant, constable of St Clement.

Continue, past a lane off to the right, on the right hand side of the road until a pavement on the other side appears. When this finishes, just beyond the corner, cross over to the gravel car park. Turn left and walk towards the telephone box at the far end.

LA ROCQUE HARBOUR

Distance:
2.25 Miles

Bus Number:
1

Toilets:
Yes

Car Parking:
Yes

Food:
No

La Platte, Rocque Point

Oyster Farm, Grouville Bay

LA ROCQUE HARBOUR

This area, which at first appears merely to be a quiet and picturesque little harbour, has played a major role in local history. It was 11pm, on the night of 5th January 1781, when a French invasion force of 1,200 men started to disembark. Under the command of the Baron de Rullecourt, a soldier of fortune with a string of unpaid gambling debts, around 600 men managed to come ashore. The falling tide denied de Rullecourt the rest of his troops and his artillery pieces. Unchallenged, they marched on St Helier, where de Rullecourt bluffed the island's governor, Moyse Corbett, into capitulating.

Fortunately not everyone was prepared to surrender. Under the command of 24 year old Major Francis Peirson, two companies of English and Scots troops, together with the Jersey Militia, attacked. In a 15 minute skirmish in the Royal Square in St Helier the French were beaten. During the battle, de Rullecourt and the hero of the hour, Pierson, were killed. Both are buried at the Town Church, de Rullecourt outside the church and Pierson inside.

Cross the slipway ahead and follow the granite sea wall. Leave the pavement as the road straightens and we walk on the roadside once more. Pass what looks like a block of 1930s apartments on the right, strangely close to a Jersey round tower; St Sampson's Tower. We catch a brief glimpse of the sea as we pass the Seymour Inn on the left before passing another Jersey round tower, Keppel Tower and, shortly afterwards, yet another. This one has had a house constructed around it. Just beyond this tower, and the nearby slipway, is a gap in the sea wall which will lead us down to a concrete platform running beside the beach. If the tide allows, descend the steps.

At the bottom of the steps turn left and walk along the concrete platform towards an imposing granite house with a round tower at its heart. Where the platform finishes, turn left, to climb the stairs to the promenade above. Here turn right. When the promenade joins the golf links, continue straight ahead along the path that runs alongside the sea wall. As we near the first German gun emplacement, look out for the golf ball set into the cement under our feet.

1. Royal Jersey Golf Club

The area on which the golf course stands is common land, which explains why we can walk here unchallenged. Thankfully nowadays, for the golfers if no one else, nobody exercises the right to graze their sheep or cattle here.

The common has long been the home of sporting endeavour. In the latter half of the 19th century horse races were held here, during a two day summer fair. Rifle shooting also regularly took place. In fact a nearby hotel, used as the clubhouse, was named the Wimbledon after the headquarters of the National Rifle Association, which was at Wimbledon in South West London.

Golf appeared in 1877, when a small band of enthusiasts got permission to mark out a few holes on the common. A club was formed a year later which established itself in a local public house. This became the Golf Inn, better known today as the Pembroke Hotel. In the early days, golfers faced two unusual hazards: sheep were still allowed to graze freely and huge piles of seaweed, drying in readiness for use as fertiliser, lined the fairways.

Two very famous golfers started their careers here: Ted Ray, who won the US Open and the British Open twice, was the descendant of a Gorey oyster fisherman, and the legendary Harry Vardon, who was brought up in a cottage beside the golf course. Vardon has the distinction of winning the US Open, the German Open and the British Open. In fact he won the British Open no less than six times!

After the second gun emplacement, continue along the sandy path beside the sea wall. Once past a raised section of antitank wall, abandon the path and bear left to skirt a hedge that surrounds an unusual property built on a Napoleonic redoubt.

On reaching the gravel track that serves this house, descend it, to enter the car park ahead through a narrow gap in the bank.

GOREY VILLAGE

Distance:
2.25 Miles

Bus Number:
1, 1b

Toilets:
Yes

Car Parking:
Yes

Food:
Café, Restaurants

GOREY VILLAGE

Leave the car park by a similar gap in the bank at the far end. Immediately turn left and then right to regain the pavement beside the main road. Look out for another, more modern, parish boundary stone set into the wall a few yards ahead.

Pass a row of charming granite cottages, then turn right briefly, to get onto the tarmac promenade that skirts the beach. Walk on towards the harbour. Near the end of the promenade, notice the shipbuilding sculpture among the gardens on the left. This serves as a memorial to the numerous boatyards that occupied the foreshore during the 1800s.

When we reach the bus shelter at the end of the promenade, turn left to cross over to the shops on the other side. Then turn left to walk towards the road that climbs ahead. Walk on for a short distance, but when the buildings end, turn hairpin right to ascend a narrow path that goes to

Mont Orgueil Castle. At the top, cross a gravel track and bear right to climb some steps onto the Castle Green. Cross the Green, heading towards the road on the left hand side, then follow it as it falls away in the distance.

Walk along the roadside for about half a mile. The pavement reappears as we leave Anne Port. The road rises and a wide pavement takes us past a disused quarry at La Crete Point. Though the pavement ends shortly, we are able to continue on the verge for a good way until we reach a hedge that skirts the road. Continue along the roadside then take a small lane, signposted Archirondel Beach and Café 100 yards, that descends towards the sea on the right. Before reaching the tarmac car park, follow a gravel track that veers off to the left and keep left to descend a slipway to the sea wall on the left.

Using care, as it can be very slippery and uneven, walk the length of the wall towards the white round tower ahead. At the end, descend the steps and cross the slipway to walk, between the beach and the tower, on the sea wall.

1. The Inshore Lifeboat

Until 1960, any coastal rescues were carried out by the lifeboat. Though it carried a small boarding boat, the difficulties of getting close enough in and the speed of rescue were a problem. Following the rescue of two men marooned on La Grande d'Azette rock in September 1959, in which the lifeboat struck a small head of rock, it was decided that a small inflatable with a powerful outboard motor would be of greater use.

The first inshore boat went into service with the States Fire Service in the spring of 1960. This was an inflatable Zodiac powered by a 40 hp outboard engine. This boat was kept, ready on its trailer, at the Fire Station in St Helier. Because it could be towed, it could get to a suitable launch site, and therefore to the incident, much faster.

It was not until 1968 that the RNLI had its own inshore boat. Following the successful rescue of four crew from the yacht Kraken, off the Dogs' Nest reef in March 1967, two of the lifeboat crew, Gerald Baudains and Gordon Coom started fundraising to buy an inshore boat for the RNLI. Sufficient funds were raised and a boat went on station at the old lifeboat house in St Helier. As the south coast was already well served by existing inshore boats, the RNLI boat was transferred to a site near St Catherine's Breakwater in 1969.

The present lifeboat house was opened in October 1990. Since June 2010 the crew has had an Atlantic 85 class lifeboat, B841, The Eric W Wilson. It carries a crew of four and has a top speed of over 35 knots from its two HO Yamaha outboard motors. It is launched from a cradle pushed into the sea by an almost submersible tractor unit. On its return, especially in rough weather, the boat is driven back into the cradle, where it is caught by restraints. During the short period that there has been a lifeboat here at St Catherine, the crew has received several citations for skill and bravery.

The footpath begins again on the sea wall beyond the next slipway. Follow the path beneath a lonely white cottage, L'Hopital, once the hospital for the workers building the breakwater. Fortunately, the two doctors who practised there were normally busy dealing with everyday ailments, rather than the horrendous injuries that the construction of a breakwater could produce. In fact, though amputations were commonplace, actual deaths were quite rare.

The path rises and, after passing through a cutting, arrives above Belval Cove. Cross the tarmac lane that runs to the beach, bear right and walk down some steps to reach the coastal path again.

Climb the steps that come in from the left, turn right and walk next to the road for a few yards. Go between some granite pillars on the right to cross a grassy barbeque area. This last short stretch of sea wall takes us to some steps which bring us out on the roadside. Here, turn right to walk towards the breakwater.

ST CATHERINE'S BREAKWATER

Distance: 1.75 Miles

Bus Number: 1b

Toilets: Yes

Car Parking: Yes

Food: Cafés, Restaurants

ST CATHERINE'S BREAKWATER

Leave the breakwater taking the road that runs to the right of the café. After 50 yards, bear right, to take the left hand footpath that climbs ahead, signposted La Ruette du Verclut footpath to Flicquet. Go up this path until we arrive at some wooden railings on the right, then turn right between the railings to follow the path ahead. On reaching the road, turn right to descend to Flicquet Bay. Ascend the narrow winding hill. Eventually it levels out and a long straight stretch takes us to a crossroads. Here turn right down La Rue du Scez. The lane bends right and then left. After the left hand bend don't turn right, but carry on straight ahead down towards Saie Harbour. The coast of France should be visible over to the right. The hill levels out and we turn left up a rough track on the left, marked La Rue des Fontenelles footpath to Rozel Hill.

1. Le Couperon Dolmen & Guardhouse

This late Neolithic, circa 3,000BC, dolmen or megalithic burial chamber is unique in two ways. First, it is one of only two of its type in the Channel Islands. It is a gallery

View towards Archirondel Tower

Scallops

Scallop Diver on St Catherine's Breakwater

chamber, which means that unlike the more common passage graves, it has no side chambers. It is not made from granite but from a stone more common in this north-eastern corner of Jersey – Rozel conglomerate or pudding stone, due to its resemblance to a plum pudding. It underwent 'restoration' by the Reverend Porter in 1868 and later by the Societe Jersiaise in 1919. What we see here at present is broadly correct, however, the porthole or kennel hole stone with the semi circular indentation in it at the eastern end of the chamber, is one of a pair that should be sited roughly half way along it. The little guardhouse, with its adjoining magazine, would have supported a battery of two 24lb cannon situated on the low hill behind the building. This battery, together with another on the headland in the distance, would have given a cross fire over Rozel Bay.

This rough track dives into a narrow valley, then turns back on itself as it winds out, up to the road at the top. When we meet the road, turn right to go down to Rozel Bay. We walk for just over a mile down this busy road. At the bottom of the hill take the middle road, that climbs slightly, to pass the archway of the Chateau La Chaire Hotel on the left.

ROZEL BAY

Distance: 3.5 Miles

Bus Number: 3

Toilets: Yes

Car Parking: Limited

Food: Cafés, Pub, Restaurants

ROZEL BAY

The road rises again; take the lane that lies in the middle, Rue du Catel, which bears right and climbs. At the summit, a glance over our left shoulder rewards us with a breathtaking view of Rozel Harbour. Continue along this lane for some way until we arrive at a lone granite house on the right hand side of the road, opposite a property called La Catel. Immediately after this house, and before the lane drops away, turn right to follow a gravel track that sweeps to the left and runs through farmland towards the sea. A sharp left brings us to a gravel car park.

Walk towards the far left hand corner of the car park and pick up the path beside the metal gate. Walk straight on and the cliff path becomes apparent, veering off to the left near a granite way mark and a wooden foot path sign.

The route along the cliff path is quite easy to follow. After half a mile the path crosses a rocky outcrop and soon after we pass a path on the left – ignore this and continue to the right on the coastal path.

Some time later the path rises and meets another wider one at right angles. Here turn right to descend towards the sea and L'Etacquerel Fort, a Napoleonic battery, that lies below. The path continues to drop until we pass through a shady glade with a stream running through it, then begins to wind its way up the hillside, finally emerging on a grassy plateau beside a secluded bungalow. Walk on, with the house on our right, then proceed straight ahead, over some wooden steps to rejoin the cliff path. Don't bear left up a wide gravel track marked Private.

Soon after, the path divides again. Here keep to the right, to descend into a small valley that has a stream and a foot bridge. Once clear of the bridge bear right to climb out of the valley. At the next summit, avoid a path that turns inland but bear right towards Bouley Bay. One final ascent up a flight of stairs and the bay lies before us.

A second flight takes us almost down to sea level. Stroll above the rocky beach for a few moments, then the path rises and weaves its way through dense woods. Just after the Water's Edge Hotel on our right, we arrive at a footpath on the right, down to Bouley Bay. Walk down the steps, and through a car park, to reach the road. At the road turn left and go up the hill for about 50 yards. On the right is a granite way mark saying Cliff Path to Bonne Nuit. Turn right up this path and ascend the steps. At the top we come out on a wide grassy track that heads inland above fields on the left. Go up the track for about 200 yards, then turn right up some steps that start next to a granite way mark. Follow the path as it runs straight ahead between fields and scrubland. The path winds and dives as we head towards Bonne Nuit. Proceed along the path into woodland. At a granite way mark, next to a finger post, turn right to descend a heavily eroded path that drops away steeply and veers slightly to the right. Near the bottom, cross rocks and approach a stream on the left. We meet a wide gravel track and see a granite way mark, Cliff path to Bonne Nuit 1982. Turn right to follow the track towards the sea.

1. Operation Hardtack 28

At 10.45pm on 24th December 1943 nine commandoes from the Special Boat Service, led by the 22 year old Captain Philip Ayton, landed here at Petit Port. Their mission was to reconnoitre this corner of the north coast, to gain intelligence and ideally take a prisoner to take back with them for questioning. They landed successfully and made their way up the path we have just come down. After about 200 yards they discovered minefield signs that faced inland, which indicated they had just crossed a minefield!

Undeterred, they pressed on to the road above. Failing to gain entry to one house, they tried another. Here they were warmly welcomed by John and Hedley Le Breton who proved to be of great assistance and told the commandoes as much as they could about the number of German troops stationed in Jersey. At around 4.45 am the next day on the way back to the rendezvous with their boat, Captain Ayton trod on a mine and was badly injured. Luckily the explosion did not alert any German troops and the party made its way back to the beach with some difficulty. The commandoes were picked up at 5.20 am.

They returned to England where, the next day, Captain Ayton died of his injuries. The memorial here recalls the raid and the loss of Philip Ayton, while a little way up the track, a wooden bench serves as a poignant memorial to the Le Breton brothers.

Leave the memorial and the fishermen's cottage, the path sweeps away to the left, as we climb some steps.

THE PATH RUNS VERY CLOSE TO THE EDGE OF THE CLIFF OVER THE NEXT FEW MILES, SO PLEASE TAKE CARE WHERE YOU WALK.

The path rises and we can see our route ahead for some distance. It then bends to the right as we approach a rocky outcrop – climb two short flights of steps and turn left to follow a wide grassy track in front of us. A few yards further up, at a signpost, bear right and climb the steps onto the path that goes to Bonne Nuit. Dodge an encroaching hawthorn and round the corner, we are rewarded with a perfect panorama of Bonne Nuit Bay in the distance. Continue on until a fork in the path, and here choose the lower path on the right and descend further.

The bay below is Giffard Bay, apparently a popular place for nude sunbathing! Above us is the island's highest point at 554ft. The radar station can be spotted there as we reach the next headland. Cross two tiny streams, then the path rises towards a sign that says No Horses or Motorcycles. On arriving at the sign we meet another path running at right angles. Turn right and follow this path as it drops away down steps before us. The path levels out and after a few steps we are at La Crête Fort.

2. La Crête Fort

Until recently this Napoleonic fort was the summer holiday home of the Lieutenant Governor, the Queen's representative in Jersey. Now it is another of the Jersey Heritage Trust's inspiring holiday lets. Originally built in 1736, as a boulevard or paved area for cannon, this defence grew into a guardhouse, then a powder magazine and finally, at the start of the 19th century, it became a fort. It was called the Havre Giffard Battery, due to its position overlooking Giffard Bay. In 1834 the fort was rebuilt to house one officer and 30 troops and was also used by the Germans during the Second World War.

Follow a wide gravel track past a modern cottage. The gravel turns to concrete as we skirt a building on the right. The track swings right and we emerge in a car park. Turn left, and ascend to the road above. Turn right and walk down the steep hill.

BONNE NUIT

Distance: 2.5 Miles

Bus Number: 4

Toilets: Yes

Car Parking: Limited

Food: Café

BONNE NUIT

Just after the bend, veer left and begin climbing again. This hill is Les Charrieres de Bonne Nuit. Walk up the hill and, about 100 yards after the bend, we reach some steps on the right. Look out for the granite way mark that says: Cliff path to La Saline. Go up the steps. At the top another breathtaking view awaits us.

1. Le Cheval Roc

In the middle of the bay stands the rocky outcrop known as Le Cheval Guilleaume, following a legend that sprang up about it. An evil sea sprite, or kelpie, who lived out in the bay had fallen madly in love with Marie, a beautiful girl from this part of St John. She, however, was already in love with a young soldier called Guilleaume. In an effort to rid himself of Guilleaume, the sprite turned himself into a stunning white charger, which Guilleaume discovered in his stable, just as he was about to depart for the wars again. Thinking it was a gift from Marie, Guilleaume rode down to Bonne Nuit expecting to see her there. As he approached the water's edge, the sprite seized his moment and galloped headlong into the waves, hoping to drown Guilleaume as he clung on to the horse's bridle. As they neared the middle of the bay, in the instant that the horse surfaced, Guilleaume managed to free himself and swim for shore, while the sprite, his magic now exhausted, turned into the rock that we see before us.

At the top, when the steps finish, follow the path to the left, as it winds through the gorse over a rocky outcrop. A level, well surfaced stretch leads us on. We pass a large building on the left, then descend some steps to regain the path.

2. The Wolf's Caves

There are caves in the cliffs below but, alas, no wolves. The caves are no longer accessible by foot, so the easiest way to see them is by boat. Even at low tide they remain waterlogged. The name could have arisen because this area is good for sea perch, also known as 'loup de la mer' or literally 'wolf of the sea'. The idea that Viking sea raiders or, wolves of the sea, landed here seems a bit tenuous. What seaman would choose to land on such a rocky shore when there are sandy beaches just around the corner?

The path rises and we pass the tall transmitter mast on our left. A long run of steps takes us back towards sea level. Where the grassy path meets a wide gravel track, turn left to go up this track as it heads inland. As we ascend, the gravel gives way to tarmac and we pass through a pair of gates. At the road, turn right to walk along a gravel pavement bordered by a chain link fence.

Walk the length of the fence and, just after the fence finishes, bear right towards a bench and a gap in the vegetation ahead. Carry on along the rough path, pass some banks of earth on the left, and make for the corner of the wooden fence in the distance. At the corner of the fence bear right to climb a shallow hill with a bench on it.

The path goes to the right of the bench, veers towards a wooden fence on the right and descends through hawthorn trees, to rise and meet the gravel pavement again. Here, bear right to continue along the pavement for a short distance.

3. The New North Road

The start of the German Occupation saw a huge rise in the number of unemployed people. The island was cut off from the rest of the world, tourists no longer arrived and import and export business stopped.

Soon over 2,000 men were out of work. It was essential that they found jobs or they might have been obliged to work for the Germans. The Department of Labour, under Deputy Edward Le Quesne, suggested that a road could be built around the coast of Jersey, to be known as Marine Drive.

The smooth, sinuously curved road we are walking along was part of that proposal. It was created entirely by human effort as no machines were used and, although there are other stretches of Marine Drive in other parishes, this is the longest.

Walk through a huge tarmac car park then, avoiding a road that goes off to the right, continue straight on along the gravel pavement ahead. The pavement rises and falls again after passing Ronez Quarries. Remain on the pavement as it bends right at the next road junction. Follow the sign post that says Sorel Point and which takes us along La Rue de Sorel. When the pavement peters out, carry on along the tarmac. About 100 yards on is a standing stone, a finger post and a sign saying Cliff paths across private property – please keep to the path. Turn left at the stone to get back on the cliff path.

We make our way to the far headland. When we reach the next one, look back to Sorel Point to see the black and white lighthouse suspended on the cliff edge and the beautiful pink granite beneath it.

After descending a few steps, the far side of Le Mourier Valley appears before us, with the path leading out running diagonally across the hill side. At the bottom, cross the gravel track and rejoin the path at the other side. Go up this path, which eventually arrives at a flat green area at the top. Here, choose the wide grass path on the extreme right that weaves its way through the gorse.

When we reach the road, beside the St Mary's Millennium Stone, turn right to go down some steps beside a granite wall.

Family of ducks on the granite causeway, Bonne Nuit Bay

DEVIL'S HOLE

Distance: 2 Miles

Bus Number: 27

Toilets: Yes

Car Parking: Yes

Food: Pub

DEVIL'S HOLE

Cross the car park, avoiding the lane on the right that leads to the Devil's Hole. At the far side of the car park in a cul de sac on the right, we find the cliff path again: Cliff Path 2 Miles to Greve de Lecq, says the sign.

Climb the steps and proceed ahead. After a few yards take a look through the trees to the right. A giant glass fibre devil stands in the pond below us. The path winds its way through a patch of vegetation and comes out on a wide gravel track. Here, turn right and follow the track for a short distance as it bends right and becomes tarmac. Walk a few steps, then bear left through a kissing gate to rejoin the cliff path.

Continue along the path, as it turns left and runs through a field, next to a rough hedgerow. It turns left again to follow a finger post and a green cliff path sign. This leads us along a wide grassy track between two narrow fields. Where this track meets another at right angles, turn right. The track bends left and we see a small reservoir below us. After about 30 yards, turn right to follow the cliff path sign. The track dips and narrows as it veers away to the right, then rises and divides. Bear right, to avoid the bridle path, and carry on past a dry stone wall and through a kissing gate. Occasionally we will see the bridle path, on our left, running parallel to us.

When we reach a National Trust for Jersey sign on the left of the path, which says Le Col de La Roc, look at the headland directly opposite us. We see a path skirting around the left hand side of a conical shaped mound. The path appears to finish at what looks like a concrete wall. Behind the wall, and just to the right of the mound, we can see a massive hole in the hill side. This is the Devil's Hole.

1. The Devil's Hole

This unusual natural feature is called a blow hole. These are formed by the gradual erosion of the roof of a cave which finally collapses. No one knows when the blow hole was formed, and until the 19th century it was called Le Creux de Vis. The origin of the present name makes an interesting tale.

It was a foul night in October 1851 when the French boat La Josephine chose to pass Jersey's north coast. She was on course from Cherbourg to St Malo with a cargo of oil. The strong current drove the boat towards the shore and, with the weather worsening, it was feared that soon she would be wrecked.

One brave sailor volunteered to swim ashore to get help but he was never seen again. By the next morning the storm had passed and the four remaining crewmen were able to scramble ashore. Left to the weather and the tide, La Josephine broke up and parts of the boat were scattered along the coastline.

Quite by chance, the figurehead of the boat was washed up inside the blow hole. The ever enterprising proprietor of the Priory public house, Nicholas Arthur, asked a local wood carver, John Giffard, to make horns, arms, a tail and a trident for the figurehead which he placed in the blow hole. Thus the name was created and the pub got a unique selling point.

The devil that we saw earlier is much more modern, being made of fibreglass. He is one of a small band – his brothers live in a warehouse in St Helier awaiting their moment of glory.

The path bears left and we ascend some steps, pass a dry stone wall and walk through a tunnel of vegetation. After a granite sign saying Crabbé 0.5 Mile Devil's Hole 1.5 Mile, we cross a stream and the path rises up to a wooden fence on the right. A few minutes later we arrive at the end of this section of cliff path.

The path climbs slightly up to a bench – here we turn left and head inland towards two granite gate posts. Continue on through these, to go along a farm track which joins another at right angles, and turn right here towards a gate.

The track bends left at the gate and goes towards a farmhouse further on. After this, Crabbé Farm, the gravel becomes a metalled road which then becomes tarmac. At the yellow line, turn right down Le Chemin du Catel. As we near the sea, the lane bends left and gets steeper, offering a superb view over Greve de Lecq Bay and the assortment of fortifications around this area. Pass the barracks on the left and, beside the Millennium Cross, cross over to the far pavement.

Looking North to Devil's Hole

GREVE DE LECQ

Distance: 2 Miles

Bus Number: 9

Toilets: Yes

Car Parking: Yes

Food: Cafés, Pubs, Restaurants

GREVE DE LECQ

Walk along the pavement, then climb some steps into the car park on the left. Cross to the car park exit, and descend the hill for a few yards to reach the tarmac lane that runs next to the granite wall of the Prince of Wales Hotel. There is a sign post: Cliff path to Plémont. Climb this steep lane which, in due course, becomes a gravel path that offers a great panorama of the beach below and the Napoleonic fort tucked into the hill side across the bay. As it levels out, the path widens into a farm track which then becomes a tarmac lane. Take the next right which is signposted Cliff Path.

The lane falls away gently, and bends between two houses. Just after the one on the right, Lecq Farm, the tarmac gives way to gravel again and we proceed on as the track rises. Where the track bends, we turn left to go down a narrow path that descends into a wooded valley.

A stream accompanies us as we head downhill. After crossing the stream, we make our way up the other side of the valley. At the top the path climbs a little more, dips and veers off to the right. Walk 100 yards or so and look out to sea – the large reef exposed at low tide is the Paternosters and the island behind it, Sark.

1. The Paternosters

In 1565, Queen Elizabeth I granted the seigneur of St Ouen, Helier de Carteret, the right to colonise Sark. Until then the island had been uninhabited and, because of this, it had often been used as a base by pirates. De Carteret chose 35 Jersey families and five Guernsey families to become the first settlers.

The boats carrying the young families left Greve de Lecq bound for Sark, visible a few miles away in the distance. On the way there, one of the boats struck Les Pierres des Lecq reef and many were drowned, among them several small children. Legend has it that their frightened cries can still be heard whenever a storm approaches.

This tale so affected the local fishermen that they always said The Lord's Prayer or the Our Father when they sailed past these rocks. Our Father in Latin is Pater Noster, and this is how the reef got its name.

The path rises and a set of steps leads down into another valley. A third valley appears, this one wider and shallower than the previous two. Once clear of this, a good stretch of level terrain rewards our previous efforts.

Soon we see the disused buildings of Plémont holiday camp on the left and the headland of La Piéce Michel, running out to sea, beneath us on the right. As we near La Piéce Michel, climb the steps and proceed over a very rough track that goes between the gorse bushes, widening as it approaches the holiday camp.

Proceed along the tarmac lane, passing two groups of three short, steel posts in the verge on the right. Pass a green holding tank on the left and continue on until we arrive at a gravel car park on the right that has a mound in the middle of it. Cross the car park to a gap in the bank, behind the mound, where a plaque says: To Plémont Beach. Walk straight down this path.

Kayaking at Gréve De Lecq

PLÉMONT

Distance: 2.5 Miles

Bus Number: 8

Toilets: Yes

Car Parking: Yes

Food: Cafés

PLÉMONT

At the bottom, the path becomes very eroded, but press on to cross a narrow road and rejoin the cliff path. There is a green and white sign that says Grosnez.

When the path levels out, a glance over to the right reveals the smooth sands of Gréve au Lanchon, or Plémont Beach. The route is relatively level for the next mile or so. After a short stretch of cement the path makes for a bench ahead. But, as we get nearer, it forks: take the left one which leads us towards the castle ruins.

Walk through the gravel car park, next to the castle ruins, then continue by going between the green way mark and the green Les Landes Site of Special Interest (SSI) sign. Follow the path as it passes to the right of a telegraph pole. The path swings to the right towards another way mark about 75 yards ahead. Here, turn right to continue along the path as it skirts the cliff. The path bends left and we can see a tall German sighting tower in the distance.

As we walk on, another way mark offers a choice of route. Here bear left to take the higher path that runs above a small quarry. As we approach a square concrete building that looks like an unfinished garage, the path forks again; take the right hand fork. Walk on and soon we meet the path coming up from the quarry.

Go down some rough steps and turn left on reaching this path. Before long we get to another set of paths, at what looks like a crossroads, here turn right towards the German tower. The path dips and rises up some shallow steps to bring us out onto a broad, flat area in front of the tower. From here, we make our way to a way mark ahead, and continue on to pass between a square bunker on the right and a gun emplacement on the left. The path veers to the left behind the gun emplacement and allows us a magnificent view of Le Pinacle, a natural megalith which suddenly appears in front of us.

1. Le Pinacle

This natural menhir has attracted man for several thousand years. When Neolithic man was putting up his own menhirs, here was one that not only dwarfed them, but was created by mother nature. It comes as no surprise then that this site was regarded with a special reverence by early man.

From Neolithic until Roman times, there is evidence of several periods of activity. The deepest excavations have revealed hearths, animal bones and round bottomed pots from the Neolithic Age. A platform, built against Le Pinacle during the Bronze Age, suggests a site used for rituals. The clearly visible foundations of a Roman fanum or temple, dedicated to pagan gods, shows that the site was still being used as late as 200 AD.

Finds of stone axes in different stages of manufacture, together with rubbing and polishing stones, lead us to believe that this may have been an area used for the large scale production of dolerite axes. The raw materials are at hand in a sill of dolerite that runs beneath the Pinacle. Furthermore, axes exported from Le Pinacle have been found in Guernsey, Alderney and Sark.

Continue to the right to skirt the cliff, another way mark can be seen ahead. Here, take the right hand path to follow the cliff edge, rather than going straight ahead.

The path rises and curves to the left. At the way mark ahead, turn right to cross the wooden bridge. Walk up the steps to the next way mark. Again we have a choice – here bear right to pass an unusual concrete shelter on the left. At the next fork, bear right again and carry on along the main path as we approach Le Pinacle on the right.

Just after Le Pinacle, we see another way mark ahead, continue on to pass it on the right then climb slightly. Stay on the path that is closest to the cliff. This bends left and right, rises and takes us to the right of a gun emplacement.

We should be able to see the south west corner of the island, La Corbière, away in the far distance, with the silhouette of another German sighting tower just piercing the horizon to the left of it. Walk around the gun emplacement and take the second path on the right to the next way mark.

BE CAREFUL HERE AS WE ARE VERY CLOSE TO THE EDGE!

The route is well defined and it is easy to see as it meanders through the gorse beside the cliff edge. In due course we pass a gun emplacement, with an old gun barrel in it, on the left. This is shortly followed by an observation post set into the cliff side on our right. The path cuts its way through the gorse towards another artillery piece, just above us and to our left.

Pass this, and another gun emplacement surrounded by green railings just beyond, then another way mark on the right. Walk towards the sandy beach in the distance and before long we see another way mark about 50 yards ahead. Pass this way mark on our right and continue on as the path descends. Another way mark presents itself; walk towards the gorse ahead as if heading for the cliff edge. As we get closer, the path becomes clearer and another way mark appears about ten yards away. A WD No14 marker lies behind it.

At this way mark, turn almost hairpin right to descend the cliff path as it heads for the road below. When we get to the road, turn right and, using care, walk down the hill to circle the rocky outcrop. We pass a lane that goes to Le Pulec beach on the right then a tiny granite cottage on the left.

L'ETACQ

Distance:
2 Miles

Bus Number:
12a

Toilets:
No

Car Parking:
Yes

Food: No

L'ETACQ

At the gravel car park, we can either walk down the slipway and carry on along the beach, or, if the tide is too high, we should continue along the road. We pass a row of cottages on the right and a lane that enters from the left. We are on Rue des Havres. Walk on past a large building with three dormer windows in the roof, then take the next right to follow Route 1 of the Cycle Network. Just before reaching the slipway, turn left to follow a narrow stretch of tarmac that runs parallel to the seashore. When this lane veers to the left, bear right and go straight on along a wide sandy track above the sea wall. The sand gives way to pebbles and the track emerges at the top of another slipway. Cross the road into a rough car park on the far side. Go through the car park to the sea wall then, using care, walk along the granite sea wall towards the building with the musket slits. Despite its appearance, this is not a Napoleonic fort – it was built as a private house.

Once past this building, when the sea wall becomes impassable, cut along the sandy path through the marram grass, going in the direction of the Martello tower in the distance. Before long we return back to the sea wall. As we near Les Laveurs slipway, the sea wall suddenly grows about four foot taller, forcing us to bear left through the dunes.

Make for the gravel car park, approximately 100 yards away on the left. When we reach the road, we can either turn right, walk down to the beach and, after turning left continue along the sands of St Ouen's Bay, or turn left, walk up to the junction, then turn right and carry on along the gravel foot path.

To walk on the sea wall, cross the gravel car park to a gap in the wooden fence, to the left of the cycle racks. Go through this gap and follow the path to pass the Martello tower and the bunker on our right. After the bunker, bear right to get back on the sea wall.

1. The Barge Aground

The Barge Aground is an icon left over from the carefree days of the 1930s. It was built in 1935 for Lionel Cox, and it was one of many seaside dwellings that lined the sea shore before the German Occupation. While the Germans tore down nearly all of these weekend homes, they kept this one and used it as a canteen.

After the war, Cox returned to the island and restored his property to its former glory. When he died in the mid 1950s, he left the Barge Aground to the Scout Association in his will.

Between 1955 and 1971, the Scout Association leased the property to a William Kerr, a research psychologist who specialised in speech disorders. He used the Barge Aground as his clinic.

When Kerr left, the Scout Association used this walled site for secure camping. In 1981, the Scout association moved its headquarters out to Clarkson Hall, a new building, built within the walls of the property. In 1997, the property was sold to the public of the island. Today the Barge

Inquisitive cattle at St Ouen

Aground is another of the Jersey Heritage Trust's exciting holiday lets.

The path beside the sea wall is quite well defined in the marram grass. Needless to say, it is best to keep a good distance from the sea wall where there are no railings, as in some places the wall is dangerously high. Proceed ahead towards another Martello tower. On our way through we cross over a German fortification and then a pebble car park. As we near the tower, walk just to the right of the bunker ahead. After the tower, we cross another rough car park to get to the promenade ahead on the right, bordered by railings. At the end of the promenade is a slipway and a large German bunker. To rejoin the promenade on the far side, turn left at the slip and go between the bunker and the café on the right. Walk along the promenade, passing an unusual white stone cottage, La Caumine à Marie Best, and a café a little further on.

2. La Caumine à Marie Best

This building, with its vaulted stone roof, was reconstructed in 1765 to serve as a powder magazine and guardhouse for the parish of St Peter. It replaced one that had earlier blown up!

After the First World War, it was turned into a weekend retreat for people who pursued the fashionable sport of surfing. Lieutenant Colonel JA Hilton acquired the property in 1932 and in 1975, his widow gave it to the National Trust for Jersey. Painted white to act as a navigation mark, the little house gets its name from the lady who lived there after it had fulfilled its military purpose.

THE WATERSPLASH

Distance:
2.5 Miles

Bus Number:
12a

Toilets:
Yes

Car Parking: Yes

Food: Bar & Restaurants

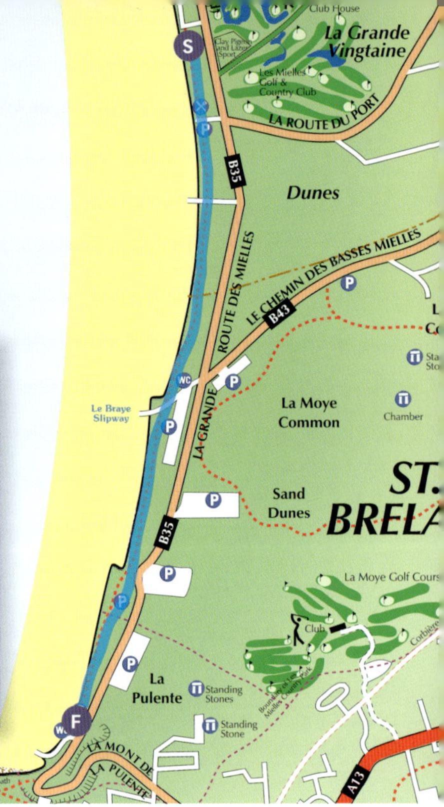

La Cobière Lighthouse from St Ouen's Bay

THE WATERSPLASH

When the promenade finishes, bear left beside the sea wall. The next slipway is Le Braye. As we get nearer, the path bends to the left, away from the sea wall. To continue on the gravel path beside the road, turn left at the slipway and, at the main road, turn right to follow the path. When this ends, continue over a short stretch of tarmac to a narrow path that runs beside the road.

To walk on the beach, descend the slip way and turn left. Once past the rocky outcrop, look out for a lone building ahead above the sea wall. This building, a public toilet, has parking and railings above it, and stands next to a cluster of conifers. Take the steps in the sea wall, then another flight of wooden steps to get to it. Cross the car parking to a narrow path that runs beside the road.

The sea wall path is the hardest option, as it is difficult to follow and the sand is very soft in places. Walk down towards the beach, then immediately after a concrete structure on the left, climb three steps and bear left to pick up the path: follow it as it heads to the far end of the bay. In due course we climb over a bunker which has an artillery piece in it. Now the route gets easier, as the path is on much firmer sand. Walk parallel to the beach for a few yards then, after passing the beach steps, bear left to climb some wooden steps up to a copse of trees. Cross the tarmac to a path that runs next to the roadside.

LA PULENTE

The narrow path rises and meets another wider gravel path at right angles. Turn right and follow this track as it rolls ahead above the beach – it bends left and climbs slightly. Avoid a narrow path on the right and carry on along this wide path as it curves to the right and descends through undergrowth. When the path emerges on to a tarmac area, turn left and climb to the road above. At the road, turn right and walk on the right, in single file if necessary. The road swoops and climbs again sharply after a small slipway set among the rocks.

Ascend the hill and, after a layby on the right, just after the bend, turn right onto a path that runs below the hotel, towards the German sighting tower.

1. La Corbière

This lighthouse, which stands at Jersey's most south westerly point, was the first reinforced concrete lighthouse built in the British Isles. Designed by the marine architect Sir John Coode and built by Imrie Bell, the light came into service in 1873. Originally powered by paraffin, it switched to electricity in the 1960s. The current strength of the beam is 1000 watts, which is visible for 18 miles. For the past 30 years there has been no lighthouse keeper, as both the light and the foghorn now run automatically.

The memorial that stands beside the road to the lighthouse proves that seafaring disasters are not always a thing of the past. It reminds us of the St Malo disaster when, on 17th April 1995, a passenger ferry, the St Malo, en route for Guernsey and Sark, struck the reefs in the foreground. Fortunately no lives were lost.

LA PULENTE

Distance: 1 Mile

Bus Number: 12a

Toilets: Yes

Car Parking: Yes

Food: Restaurants

LA CORBIERE

Distance:
2.5 Miles

Bus Number:
12

Toilets:
Yes

Car Parking: Yes

Food: Restaurant

LA CORBIERE

On reaching the car park at the side of the tower, cross to the gap in the bank in the far corner. We pass an SSI sign and a way mark. Walk towards a building in the far distance which looks like a golf ball – this is a weather radar station – then bear left towards a large building with a green roof. By now, the footpath should be easier to make out as it skirts the cliff edge.

Pass one way mark on our right and, at the next one, turn sharp right to go down some steps that lead towards the rocky beach below. Follow the path as it goes around the beach then, on reaching a wide grassy area, turn left to climb a tall flight of steps that takes us back up the cliff. After passing a tiny quarry on the right, the path climbs further and veers to the right. At the top, continue along a broad track that goes to a granite building ahead. Pass this on our left, and continue straight on, descending gradually between the gorse bushes. Bear right when the path forks some way on.

We should see a chain link fence and concrete posts about 100 yards ahead of us – walk towards these. As we approach the fence, we will see a way mark. Turn right here and walk beside the fence to reach a railway track just below. Using care, as it is normally slippery here, walk down the railway track until it gets to a concrete path on the left. Turn sharp left here and make for some steps ahead. At the top of these steps, turn right and then left after a few paces, to climb another run of steps. The path rises and curves to the left.

Cross a tarmac drive and continue on the wide track that lies behind the gate. Follow this wide, uneven track as it meanders towards the 'golf ball'. It veers to the left and heads inland, passing a wooden fence as it does so. As we draw level with the radar station, we see a short granite pillar, set in concrete, on the right of the path. Turn right here to carry on along the well worn path that runs around the perimeter fence of the weather station. On reaching an open area, in front of the gates, turn left to walk along a track that runs through the gorse towards the high security fence of HM Prison La Moye.

La Rocco Tower and La Corbière Lighthouse

The track emerges on a tarmac and concrete lane. Turn right to go towards the sea. Avoiding a Private Road, follow the lane as it bends left and right. Just before a house called The Old Signal Point, bear left onto a gravel path which is way marked.

The path is well used and simple to follow. Keep straight on, avoiding one to the Old Quarry. The path falls away down steep steps, nearly to sea level, then climbs again after a brief beachside diversion. Back on high ground, we return onto gravel. We pass a wall on the left and head through a junction where five paths meet. In front of us, in a clearing, stands a large pillar which is engraved La Grosse Tete. At the pillar, bear left to follow the path as it approaches a car park in the distance. Go down the path and, when it splits, turn left to go through the wall into Beauport car park.

To leave the car park, walk a few yards along the tarmac to a finger post and way mark which says St Brelade's Church. Turn right here. The path dips into a glade and rises to skirt an uncultivated field. After winding through undergrowth, it descends down a very eroded set of steps to come out on the road. Here, turn left, passing the cemetery and then St Brelade's Church on the seaward side. At the T junction, next to the War Memorial, turn right and walk along the road for about 200 yards.

1. St Brelade's Church

This beautiful 11th century church is named after a Celtic saint, St Brelade or Bramwalader. Like most parish churches in the island, it has grown and seen many changes. The Reformation brought austerity to the church; the altar disappeared, as did the statues, the font and the stained glass. The font was discovered three centuries later in the undergrowth above the church.

Fortunately before the Reformation, the small chapel at the side of the church, The Fishermen's Chapel, had been turned into a home for the two cannons that the parish kept for defence. It is due to this that the wall paintings, which date from the early 15th century, still exist today.

The interior of the church was restored in 1895 by Reverend AJ Balleine. During the restoration, the plaster on the walls and ceiling of the church was removed, exposing the warm pink La Moye granite and the odd beach pebble complete with attached limpet!

ST BRELADE'S BAY

Distance: 2 Miles

Bus Number: 12

Toilets: Yes

Car Parking: Yes

Food: Cafés, Restaurants, Pubs

ST BRELADE'S BAY

Pass the St Brelade's Bay Hotel and, shortly afterwards, go down some steps on the right that lead to the promenade; turn left and proceed along it. If the tide allows, walk across the beach towards the cliffs. At the end of the promenade, climb the steps to go over the headland. At the far side, follow the path as it runs beside the sea wall. At the slipway, turn right towards the beach, then immediately left to walk on an uneven concrete platform alongside the sea wall.

Cross a short section of rocky beach, then climb up on the left to get to the start of the cliff path. It is signposted Public footpath to Portelet Common. Go up this steep path, through the quarry and up the steps to arrive on Portelet Common. At the top of the steps, turn right and head towards a granite memorial, surrounded by a circle of boulders.

The National Trust for Jersey

The Trust was set up in 1936 by a group of islanders who felt that Jersey was becoming over-run with speculative building. Even then the island's coastline and valleys were under threat and, had it not been for the far sightedness of this small group of people, much of what we hold dear today would have been lost. The first piece of land purchased was an area in Vallee des Vaux, which was likely to be sold for building. This tranquil wooded site was purchased by Carlyle Le Gallais, a founder member of the Trust, who gave it to the Trust upon its incorporation in 1937.

At present the Trust owns over 150 sites, either as properties or land and, as such, it is one of the largest landowners in the island, owning 2% of Jersey.

The tiny building on the headland on the right was the powder magazine that supported La Cotte Battery on the other side of the headland. This was built in 1759. It and Le Coleron Battery, on the far side of the bay, provided a cross fire over St Brelade's Bay. After the threat of war had passed, the building was used by workmen excavating the quarry below and it even had a tenant in more recent times.

With St Brelade's Bay on the right, walk through the circle of stones towards a wall in the distance. Just below us and slightly to the left, we can see the path ahead. Follow the path as it makes for a wall, about 200 yards in the distance. Near the wall, turn left and pick up the path as it runs parallel to the wall for some distance. Pass the entrance to the nature reserve on our right, and veer left to continue along a wide track that runs under the trees. This track passes through a gate, then bears right across a rough surface. At the end of the hedge on the right, turn right to get onto a tarmac lane. Walk up this lane, passing the Portelet Hotel on the left, then turn next right into Rue Voisin. After 100 yards the lane bends to the right. Here turn left into a lane marked Private Road – No Through Road.

St Brelade's Parish Church and Fisherman's Chapel

OLD PORTELET INN

Distance: 2 Miles

Bus Number: 12

Toilets: Yes

Car Parking: Yes

Food: Restaurant, Pub

Command Bunker, Noirmont Point

Janvrins Tomb, Portlet Bay

OLD PORTELET INN

Walk through this short stretch of road to pass the Old Portelet Inn on the left. Soon after, we arrive at a large gravel car park on the right. Cross the car park to the far right hand corner where the path starts again. Continue along the path, crossing over another wider path at right angles, to go towards a gun emplacement ahead; after this, we turn right to go along the road towards the headland.

1. Noirmont Point

German Forces landed in Jersey on 1st July 1940 and five long years of occupation began. The invaders met no resistance; the British army had pulled out a week or so earlier, preventing the bloodbath that occurs when soldiers and civilians mix on the battlefield. In October 1941, Hitler gave orders that the islands should be turned into 'an impregnable fortress', and this corner of Jersey proves that beyond any doubt. Each of the four raised gun platforms housed 150mm naval guns, manned by naval personnel and taken from First World War battleships. The battery is named after one of them; the SMS Lothringen. The tall tower on the cliff edge controlled the battery and behind each slit in the tower's wall was a crew dedicated to range finding for one of the guns above.

Leave the headland by following the path that goes just to the left of the closest gun emplacement (avoid a path on the right that goes down to the sea). The path turns left and crosses a rocky outcrop. Go straight ahead, passing two paths that go off to the left. When the path forks again, bear right as it rises and curves to the right. Within yards we arrive at a chain link fence; the path turns left here to run beside the fence for about half a mile, so carry on alongside the fence, which is straight for quite a distance before turning sharp left. Continue on beside the fence, ignoring any paths that enter from the left.

Finally the path and fence turn right and, after a short distance, the path bears left towards a way mark at the roadside. At the road, turn right to go through a crossroads and carry on along La Route de Noirmont. Take the next right into the Green Lane; La Rue de Haute. The lane is level for around a mile, then it gets steeper as it twists and turns down to the sea. Ignore a turning on the left when the lane straightens out and continue down Mont es Tours. The hill bends sharply to the left and becomes Mont de Boulevard. At the bottom, turn left and continue along the pavement. When this ends, near the National Westminster bank, cross the road to go in front of St Brelade's Parish Hall.

2. St Aubin's Village

Like many other coastal villages, St Aubin takes its name from the 6th century bishop of Angers, who was said to give protection from pirates. This is rather ironic, as Jersey's highly successful fleet of privateers was based here during the English Civil War.

Before the harbour at St Helier was built, St Aubin was the main port for Jersey. It lay sheltered from the south-west gales behind Noirmont Point and the firm sands allowed boats to unload their cargo directly into carts drawn up alongside. The port prospered and the wealthy merchants put up elegant houses on the quayside to be on hand when their ships returned. The long narrow gardens of these houses show how much land has been reclaimed from the sea. In those days there was no road around the bay from St Helier, so everything was carried across the beach by horse and cart. In fact the island's first bus service was a horse and cart that ran across the sands from St Helier to St Aubin.

By 1844, a road finally joined La Haule to St Aubin. At that time the boat building industry was booming and ships, as large as The Evening Star at 800 tons, were often seen on the seashore. At about the same time a railway company was formed with the idea of running a line out from the town. This eventually came to fruition in 1870, when a train running through the dunes and shipyards arrived at St Aubin among great celebrations.

Today St Aubin's harbour is packed with pleasure craft. The merchants, the boat building and the train have vanished but, even without all this, the village is still as vibrant and inviting as ever.

ST AUBIN'S VILLAGE

Distance: 3 Miles

Bus Number: 12, 12a,15

Toilets: Yes

Car Parking: Yes

Food: Cafés, Restaurants, Pubs

St Brelade's Parish Hall,
St Aubin's Harbour

ST AUBIN'S VILLAGE

Walk in front of the Parish Hall and then bear left to go between it and the toilets on the right. From here simply walk around the bay, along the beach side promenade, to the town, which can be seen beneath the granite fortifications on the far hill.

As we near the finish we pass a large area of grass on the left, beyond the dual carriageway and the Grand Hotel also on the left. Just after the hotel, turn left to pass to the left of the upturned boat café, La Fregate.

Follow the pink tarmac towards the Radisson Hotel on the corner. Here turn left and walk on to the far corner of the marina. At the corner, turn right to follow the railings around the marina, then take the first on the left and carry on beside the road until the roundabout. There, turn right and follow the pavement back to the Elizabeth Terminal.

Section 2 - **GUERNSEY**

Again, the distances between these suggested stops vary, so approximate mileages have been given. All 17 points are accessible by bus, but please check the timetable, and most have car parking and toilet facilities (although there is limited opening of public toilets in the winter). There are usually cafés or kiosks, public houses or restaurants open nearby, but again check before setting out.

Some useful phone numbers

The dialling code for Guernsey is 01481. Five digit information lines cannot be called from mobile phones.

Guernsey Information Centre	Telephone: 723552
Guernsey Bus Service	Telephone: 720210/12021
Weather Forecast	Telephone: 12080

In an emergency dial 112 or 999

Although the coast is not short of places to stop for refreshment, it is wise to carry water and a snack. A mobile phone is also a good idea, but remember that you might not always get a signal. A bus timetable and a tide table can be very useful too.

Where there is no pavement, in most cases, it is safest to walk on the right hand side of the road in single file.

Finally, the island has one of the largest and fastest ranges of tide in the world, so make sure that you can cross a beach without becoming trapped by the incoming tide. Please be aware of the tide at all times, particularly when walking on the causeway to Lihou Island.

Suggested stops

1 LIBERATION MONUMENT
Car Parking, Public Toilets, Cafés, Restaurants, Pubs, All Bus Routes

2 JERBOURG POINT
Car Parking, Public Toilets, Kiosk, Hotel, Bus Route 6

3 ICART POINT
Car Parking, Public Toilets, Kiosk, Hotel, Bus Route 6/6a

4 PETIT BÔT BAY
Car Parking, Public Toilets, Café, Bus Route 4 or 7/7a – ask driver for nearest stop and walk there

5 LES TIELLES CAR PARK
Car Parking, Bus route 7/7a – ask driver for nearest stop and walk there

6 PORTELET SLIPWAY, PLEINMONT
Car Parking, Public Toilets, Kiosk, Hotel, Bus Route 7/7a

7 L'ERÉE
Car Parking, Public Toilets, Café, Restaurant, Hotel, Bus Route 7/7a, 5/5a

8 VAZON BAY (SOUTH)/ RICHMOND KIOSK
Car Parking, Public Toilets, Kiosk, Bus Route 7/7a

9 VAZON BAY CAFE (NORTH)
Car Parking, Public Toilets, Café, Restaurant, Bus Route 7/7a, 3/3a

10 COBO
Car Parking, Public Toilets, Kiosk, Hotel, Tearoom, Pub, Fish and Chip Shop, Bus Route 7/7a, 3/3a, 2

11 LES GRANDES ROCQUES
Car Parking, Public Toilets, Kiosk, Pub, Hotel, Bus Route 7/7a, 3/3a

12 PORT SOIF
Car Parking, Public Toilets, Kiosk, Bus Route 7/7a, 3/3a

13 ROUSSE
Car Parking, Public Toilets, Kiosk, Pub, Hotel, Bus Route 7/7a

14 CHOUET
Car Parking, Public Toilets, Kiosk, Café, Bus Route 6/6a, 7/7a (seasonal) – ask driver for nearest stop and walk there

15 L'ANCRESSE BAY
Car Parking, Public Toilets, Kiosks, Restaurant/Café, Bus Route 6/6a, 7/7a (seasonal)

16 BORDEAUX HARBOUR
Car Parking, Public Toilets, Kiosk, Bus Route 6/6a, 7/7a (seasonal)

17 BELLE GREVE BAY
Car parking, Public Toilets, Café, Bus Route 6/6a, 7/7a, 8/8a

Fort Grey, Rocquaine

LIBERATION MONUMENT

Distance: 4 Miles

Bus Number: All routes to Bus Terminus

Toilets: Yes

Car Parking: Yes

Food: Cafés, Restaurants, Pubs

LIBERATION MONUMENT

The route starts in Guernsey's capital, St Peter Port, next to the Liberation Monument and clock tower, and opposite the White Hart public house. Head south, past a small street on the right and the Guernsey Information Centre towards Victoria Pier (otherwise known as the Crown Pier). Walk beside the marina past the Albion House public house and the Town Church, following the footpath as it weaves its way around the Albert Memorial.

1. The Town Church

This is often regarded as the finest in the Channel Islands and, like all local Norman churches, it has grown over the centuries. Though it is difficult to date accurately, we know that Duke William of Normandy, later William the Conqueror, gave the church to the Abbott of Marmoutier in 1048. It was common for Norman abbeys to have land in the Channel Islands and, after the Conquest, this continued for 300 years or so, until Henry V initiated the Suppression of the Alien Priories. When this happened, most of the monks returned to their mother houses in France and their churches fell into disrepair.

In those days, the churchyard extended to the sea on its eastern side, and half way along Market Street to the west. The southern part of the churchyard was the cemetery.

The church we see today is principally the result of two major restorations; one which took place in 1826 conducted by the architect John Wilson, and one in 1866 by Harry Hems. Before these, the west aisle had been home to the militia cannon, a common practice in Channel Island churches, and the north transept was the location of the States' fire engine. Above all this was a consistory court room, which until 1858, had jurisdiction over matrimonial and probate matters.

The more observant will notice that much of the stained glass is relatively new. This is because during June 1944, a US aircraft bombed the old harbour and the blast blew out the church windows.

Walk on beside the Albert Marina, opposite the Bus Terminus, and cross the Castle Pier. Continue along the South Esplanade, next to Havelet Bay, towards the foot of the hill ahead, Le Val des Terres. Fork left to follow the road that runs beside the sea shore. Castle Cornet dominates this deep water anchorage. Look out for the seawater bathing pools that line the shore.

2. Castle Cornet

The castle stands on an islet to the south of the town of St Peter Port. Like its counterpart, Mont Orgueil in Jersey, building began at the beginning of the 13th century when King John lost his lands in France and the islands suddenly became a frontier outpost of England.

As well as guarding the town, the other purpose of the castle was to safeguard ships anchored beneath its walls. For many years, Guernsey was a vital staging point on the wine route from Bordeaux to Southampton.

The waters around the castle have provided both a defence and more importantly a lifeline.

Because Castle Cornet could be provisioned by boat, it has withstood some lengthy sieges, for example between 1338 and 1345, when the castle was in the hands of the French. During this siege, the French strengthened the castle; they added the Barbican built outside the 13th century entrance to the inner ward. Later, in the 17th century, the island's Governor, Sir Peter Osborne, retired into the castle and declared his support for King Charles, while the rest of the island supported Oliver Cromwell. On this occasion the defenders held out for eight and a half years before a fleet under Admiral Blake forced their surrender.

In 1672, the castle's 40ft high keep was struck by lightning; at the time it was being used as the powder magazine. The resulting explosion cost the lives of seven people, including the Governor's wife and her mother. It destroyed the keep, the Governor's residence and the buildings around the central courtyard.

When we reach the Aquarium, bear left and climb the steps following the signs to

Castle Cornet, Havelet Bay

Fermain and South Coast. Go through the arch, to pass the Clarence Battery on the left. Turn right and, keeping left, head up the hill beneath the walls of Fort George, towards Fermain Bay and St Martin's Point. Carry on along this path, avoiding the turning to Soldiers' Bay.

3. Fort George

This impressive Napoleonic fort was built because Castle Cornet was no longer a match for the artillery power of the day. Built between 1782 and 1812, on the hill that overlooks the town and harbour of St Peter Port, this defence covered 48 acres. It was made up of a star-shaped citadel, brick built with a dry moat around it, Fort Irwin, and eight batteries: Adolphus, Charlotte, Kent, Town Point, York, Fausse Braye, Belvedere, and – standing on Les Terres Point, overlooking Havelet Bay – the outlying Clarence Battery.

In 1807, the island garrison stood at around 4,000 men, most of whom were stationed at Fort George. During the Second World War the citadel became the headquarters of the German Luftwaffe radar defences. It was heavily bombed by the RAF in 1944 before the Allied invasion of Normandy. The site was purchased by the States of Guernsey in 1958 and sold to developers in 1961. It is now an up-market housing estate.

When we emerge onto tarmac, bear left and continue, regaining the coastal path by going through a barrier on the left, just after the turning point in the road. The wall that we pass on the right is the Adolphus Battery, an outwork of Fort George. Ascend some shallow steps. Go up another set of steps on the left and then descend to a junction in the path. Here, turn left, en route for Fermain Bay.

Go down some more granite steps, and past another way mark, which takes us through some cast iron posts, and descend further. After the path narrows and drops again, carry straight on.

When we reach a crossroads, where steps climb both straight on (to Fermain Bay), and to the right, turn left, taking steps towards 'Moorings'. Notice the way mark on the left at ground level. At the red and white navigation mark, continue on to Fermain Bay. We'll see a way mark on the right. The path rises with granite steps and we pass a way mark for St Martin's Point. Continue on up.

At the next junction, ignore the right turn, but turn hairpin left following a way mark that says Bay. Descend more steps and another hairpin to reach Fermain Bay.

4. Fermain Bay

This beach is popular because of its sheltered position. For sailors it offers a safe anchorage, and an easy place to come ashore. It's hardly surprising then, that in 1842, when the British government was looking to build 'harbours of refuge', in reality huge naval bases for the British Fleet, Fermain Bay was its chosen location in Guernsey.

The plans for the harbour in Guernsey were abandoned, but work went ahead on the other two harbours; at Braye in Alderney and at St Catherine's Bay in Jersey. Progress on both harbours was slow and neither harbour was ever finished.

The stream that forms the boundary between the parishes of St Martin's and St Peter Port runs down the valley and meets the sea here. In Edwardian times, decorum forced bathers to be segregated, gentlemen occupying one side of the beach and ladies the other.

Pass the café and the loop-holed tower; go over the small bridge to rejoin the coastal path, then ascend the steps ahead. Note the way mark that says St Martin's Point. Soon our efforts are rewarded with a great view over Fermain Bay. Proceed ahead, take the next left and descend the steps, where the way mark says Bec du Nez and Marble Bay. Do not go straight on.

Climb the windy path and continue towards St Martin's Point. Further on, beside the bench, turn left and go down steps that lead to Marble Bay.

The path drops down to a rocky outcrop and rolls away to the right between pine trees. Cross the wooden bridge and walk on towards the pines. Go straight on at the next junction to pass a set of steps on the right. The path rises and falls. At the fork, turn right and ascend the steps, then bear right and continue up towards the bunker. Here, go straight up, not left. At the top we're in Jerbourg Point car park, almost 300ft above sea level.

Fermain Bay

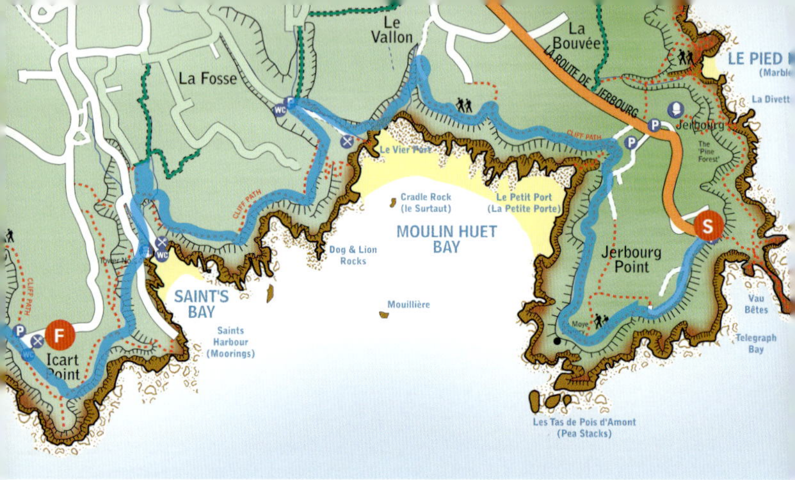

JERBOURG POINT

Leave the car park at its left corner, closest to the coast, where we see the way mark, Cliff Path to Petit Port. Follow the lane, bearing left at the fork to continue alongside the coast then rejoining the path. Continue until the sign for the RSPB bird hide and bear right. We come to a cliff side memorial to Victor Gosselin Carey, who was Bailiff of Guernsey between 1935 and 1946. The cliffs here were given to the island by Mr Carey's two sons in 1959.

Take the middle of the three paths, just to the left of the bench. After a sharp descent, climb up to the lane ahead. Turn left and continue. Take the second path on the left, cutting through the bank, then soon afterwards turn right and go up a short rise. Soon we arrive at a large bunker. Look out for the way mark on the left that says Petit Port Bay; turn left here and follow the path. We meet a concrete path, so turn left and continue, go down a few steps, turn right through a barrier, and head for Moulin Huet. Note the way mark on the right.

Take the left fork and drop down a few steps, staying on the public path until we reach some steps with a railing. Go up turning left at the top onto a narrow road. The road drops and, at the bottom, we need to turn hairpin left towards the barrier ahead. On our left we pass an abreuveur (stone water trough).

We are accompanied by a stream for a short distance. Before long we pass through a barrier to emerge on a road. The way mark beside the path says Moulin Huet; Saint's Bay and Icart Point. Turn hairpin left and descend the lane towards Moulin Huet. Just after a cottage, we come to a bench and a railing, turn right, to follow the way mark Saint's Bay and Icart Point, and climb the steps. At the T junction, turn left and make for Saint's Bay. Climb some more steps, and at the next T junction turn left again. Here we are 260ft above sea level. Don't turn right to Hotel Bon Port but go straight on, passing a memorial.

After passing a gate, the path splits. Bear left immediately after the bench, go through a barrier and, at the road, turn left then bear right towards Saint's Harbour. Ignore the cliff path on the right that goes to Icart Point. We pass a loop-holed tower. The closeness of the road to the tower, and the similarity in height suggests that the road was built well after the threat of invasion. When the road ends, go up the steps on the right following a way mark to Icart Point.

Ascend the steps and pass Saint's Bay Battery, one of two that would have fired across the bay. At the top, when we meet the path again, follow the way mark and turn left towards Icart Point. Ignore a right turn and proceed ahead.

JERBOURG POINT and ICART POINT

Distance: 4.5 Miles (Jerbourg-Icart 3 Miles) (Icart-Petit Bôt 1.5 Miles)

Bus Number: Jerbourg 6, Icart 6, 6a

Toilets: Yes

Car Parking: Yes

Food: Kiosk, Hotel

ICART POINT

On reaching the car park, head for the way mark on the right in front of us. This one says to Jaonnet Bay, Petit Bôt, Le Gouffre and Pleinmont Point. Go straight ahead, over the concrete, towards the benches. We come to a T junction, so turn right and follow the path as it goes around to the left.

As we climb avoid a grassy path on the right and continue ahead. When the path forks, take the right, follow the path, then descend steps to a T junction. Turn left and go down some more steps. On reaching the road, turn left and walk down to Petit Bôt Bay.

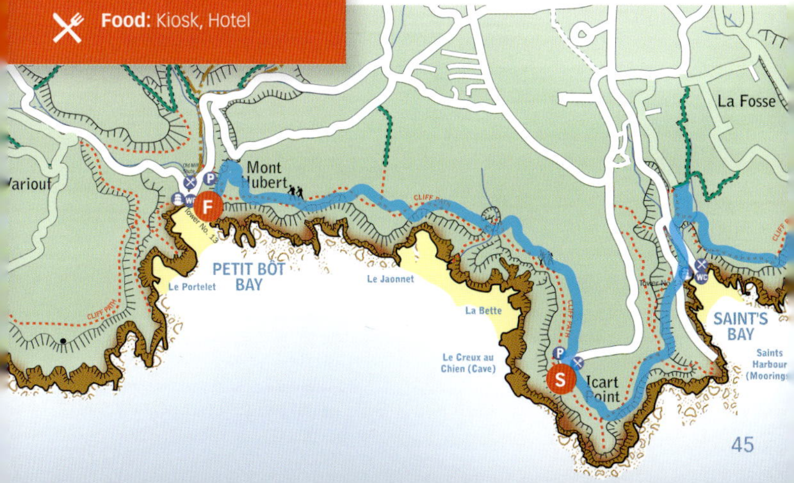

PETIT BÔT BAY

Distance: 4.5 Miles

Bus Number: 4, 7/7a – will need to walk from main road

Toilets: Yes

Car Parking: Yes

Food: Café

PETIT BÔT BAY

Continue on down to the slipway and around the café. Then head back inland for a few metres to some concrete steps on the left. Climb to rejoin the coastal path; the way mark on the right says Portelet and Le Gouffre. At the next junction continue on towards the battery and then go down the steps towards the guard house. When near the battery, turn right to climb the steps. At the top turn right, away from Portelet, and then immediately left back onto the path.

After the barrier, stay on a wide track that runs off to the left for about half a mile, then turn left to follow a granite way mark – Cliff Path. Descend steps into a wooded valley with an ancient abreuveur (stone trough) on the right. At the junction ahead we meet a path that runs alongside an old wall, turn left here.

Descend the steps towards the point. When the path divides, bear right, between a granite wall and an outcrop of rock. Ignore the steps on the left. Just before the café/restaurant, turn left to follow the sign for Pleinmont. Continue on, passing an abreuveur with a well head which, at nearly 280ft above sea level, is quite high for a spring. Continue on, following the way mark, to Le Bigard.

When the coastal path finishes, beside a private house, carry on up the paved driveway and when the tarmac joins a rough track bear left. Continue until we arrive at a hairpin bend on a public road, again bear left. At the foot of the incline, turn hairpin left onto a broad path which is way marked La Corbière footpath. Go through a pair of green bollards. Stay on this broad track and head for the pine trees ahead, but before reaching them, cut through a gap in the bank on the left to cross an open area of grass. Go past the memorial stone and at the fork, bear left. Keep left. As we drop down, a fabulous view of the coastal rocks can be seen. We pass a bench dedicated to Lt Col SC McCartney, chairman and president of the National Trust of Guernsey 1967-1973.

1. The National Trust of Guernsey

The Trust was formed in 1960 and has its HQ at 26 Cornet Street, St Peter Port. It owns more than 75 'properties', some of these you will walk along around the different parts of the island. The first of these was an area of land at Pleinmont, Le Vaux de Monel, given to the Trust by Miss May Bonamy-Collings in June 1961. From the slopes of that wooded valley, there is a superb panorama of Rocquaine Bay and Fort Grey.

Other sites owned by the Trust include land in the Talbot Valley, and Le Catioroc at the south end of Le Chemin le Roi. The Trust also runs the Folk & Costume Museum at Saumarez Park. In 1974, the National Trust of Guernsey invited Mr CEB Brett to make a survey of the buildings in St Peter Port. He was assisted by a number of local researchers and his report was published in 1975. So well was it received that the Alderney Society asked him to produce a similar document for them. This came out in 1976, followed in 1977 by a survey of St Helier for the National Trust for Jersey.

At the open area bear left and follow the path and, when it splits again, keep left. The path climbs and at the T junction, turn left. Go past two paths on the right. After descending over some rocks, and passing through a barrier, we arrive on a rough tarmac track. Avoiding a right turn, walk straight on towards a car park.

Cross the car park, making for the far right-hand corner, where we pick up the path again. The path is way marked

South Coast Cliff Path

Le Bigard

View across fields towards Torteval Church

Prevôte and Pleinmont Point. After going down a short flight of steps, turn right and go down a few more. We are dropping into a small valley, and in the distance we can see the path snaking along the other side of it. When the path levels out, proceed on. After the steps, bear right to follow the arrows to Pleinmont and the main cliff path. The tall building ahead is La Prevôté Tower.

2. La Prevôté Tower

The first tower built here went up at the instigation of Sir John Doyle, during the Napoleonic era. It was built to guard the Hâvre de Bon Repos. One might think that the precipitous cliffs in this area would deter most potential invaders, but Doyle thought otherwise. He had watch towers built here, and further westward around the coast, at Les Tielles, Mont Hérault and Pleinmont. Where there was a possible landing site, such as Fermain Bay, Saints Bay and Petit Bôt Bay, he put up a tower and ramparts.

The tower was built during the Second World War and is made of reinforced concrete. This tower is unique, in that it was built by the German Army rather than the Navy, which built all the other ones.

At the tower, bear right, to walk through the quarry, to the car park below. There, turn right and carry on along the road, and take the first left onto the coastal path. Notice the way mark: Pleinmont Point. We drop into a small valley and, after climbing the steps, go straight on, disregarding a path on the right. Ahead and to the left, at sea level, we can see the sea cave at Le Creux Mahié.

3. Le Creux Mahié

This is the largest cave along Guernsey's 38 mile coastline. It is around 200 ft long, 40 to 50 ft wide and up to 60 ft high.

In days gone by, guides would illuminate the cave by lighting fires of dried furze. It is said that the walls of the cave are still black with the soot from these fires.

Local folklore says that at night fairies emerge from the cave to dance and cavort on the cliff tops, or that the cave is the entrance to a long tunnel that goes to St Saviour's Church, almost two miles away.

A challenging series of roller coaster descents and climbs finally rewards us with a lengthy section of flat path. Just before the next barrier, don't turn left but continue on to a T junction. Here turn left towards Pleinmont. When we come to a fork, keep right to pass a lonely bit of brick wall. In the distance we can see the spire of Torteval Church.

LES TIELLES CAR PARK

Distance: 4.5 Miles

Bus Number: 7/7a – ask driver and walk there

Toilets: No

Car Parking: Yes

Food: No

LES TIELLES CAR PARK

We come to a small car park, cross it and follow the way mark to Mont Hérault and Pleinmont. We are very close to the cliff edge, but fortunately a chain link fence separates us from the 260 ft drop to the sea beneath. The cove that lies on our left is called Belle Elizabeth.

1. Belle Elizabeth

Legend has it that a beautiful young girl called Elizabeth leapt to her death here, because her parents had forbidden her to marry her lover. In the style of all good legends, it is said that one of the offshore rocks is her petrified remains.

We go past a deserted granite building sitting directly on the point. This is the Mont Hérault watch house, built in 1804. It is one of a chain of buildings erected on the coast to give warnings of enemy activity. Once past this, we are able to see a Second World War German range-finding tower and a modern day radio beacon. When the coastal path finishes, turn left onto a track which will take us towards the road. Just before reaching the tarmac, fork left onto a gravel track. When this track bends to the right, go straight ahead to follow the way mark that says Cliff Path; here the path drops down some steps into a shallow valley. Look out for the deep narrow sea inlet on the way to the range-finding tower and bunker ahead. The tower looks intimidating, looming above us on the high ground.

2. L'Angle Tower MP4

Possibly the most impressive range-finding tower in the islands, this one is unlike all the others. Instead of being round, this tower is rectangular and in two sections. It has three levels in the upper section and two levels in the lower. Each level would have controlled one of the five naval batteries originally planned for Guernsey.

Only three naval batteries were built, and the army were given the other two levels for their batteries. In the latter stages of the war, a Freya radar was mounted on the top of the tower.

Go past this bunker and a further two before reaching a car park. The coastal path carries on directly across this.

Make your way towards the gun battery and radio tower in the distance. On our right, we can see a restored artillery piece, part of Batterie Generaloberst Dollman.

3. Batterie Generaloberst Dollman

The German Second World War batterie that we see here was made up of four 22 cm Schneider K534 guns, each housed in a separate gun pit and guided by the range finding tower on the headland. They could fire a 22 cm round a distance of 22 km, at the rate of a round every minute. The batterie was fully operational by December 1941, and was manned by men of the 15th Battery of the IV Battalion of 1265 Artillery Regiment.

The four guns used here were made for the French Army during the First World War by Schneider et Cie, at Le Creusot, France. Sixty eight of these guns were captured by German troops during their advance into France at the beginning of the Second World War. In 1941, when extra guns were needed to defend Hitler's Atlantic Wall, they were retrieved and put into use again. Of the 40 used for coastal defence, 16 could be found in the Channel Islands.

The restored gun emplacement is the work of Guernsey Armouries. Over the course of four years, over 1,000 tons of spoil was dug out, steelwork was shot-blasted and repainted, and camouflage applied in the original colours. The gun that we can see has a genuine barrel, lifted from the base of cliffs at Les Landes in Jersey, and a replica chassis and cradle made using the original blueprints from the French Ministry of Defence.

Quite soon we arrive at another car park which marks the beginning of the Pleinmont Nature Reserve. Walk on. On a clear day we should see the Hanois Lighthouse offshore. If it is foggy we will definitely hear it!

4. Les Hanois Lighthouse

In the period between 1835 and 1862, before Trinity House built the Hanois Lighthouse, almost 100 ships had become wrecked or stranded on Guernsey's rocky coastline. One of the more notable ships that perished was the frigate HMS Boreas, which went down on 7th December 1807 with the loss of 154 lives.

The Hanois Lighthouse stands on Le Biseau Rock, about a mile off Guernsey's south western corner. Made of

Les Hanois Lighthouse at sunset

interlocking blocks of Cornish granite, which were dressed on the Castle Cornet breakwater and brought around to the rock in barges, it rises 117ft above the water line. The foundation stone was laid on 15th August 1860, and the light shone for the first time on 8th December 1862. Nowadays electricity, generated on site, powers a beam which is visible for 16 miles.

Like most lighthouses, the Hanois now runs automatically, so no longer do keepers have to come out in a small boat from Portelet Harbour at Pleinmont to tend to the light. The lighthouse keepers' cottages are across the road from the harbour, just out of sight of the lighthouse. Before radio or telephone became available, the keepers' wives would communicate with their husbands by flag from La Varde Rock, a tall promontory just to the west of the cottages.

We can see Pleinmont Second World War Naval Observation Tower (open to the public on selected days) ahead of us. The path turns, goes up some steps and we enter another car park. With the tower on our right, the coastal path starts again

Pleinmont Observation Tower

on the far side of the car park. Shortly after leaving it, turn left down the steps, following the sign on the way mark that says Cliff Path, Portelet, Bus Terminus. After the steps, the path descends further. Ignore a path on the left and go straight ahead. The path turns to the right and opens out before joining tarmac. On the way we pass an ancient stone circle, known as the Fairy Ring or, more correctly, La Table des Pions.

5. La Table des Pions

This is a circular area of grass, surrounded by a shallow trench, itself enclosed by a ring of stones. This is where the Pions, or young valets, would sit to eat a meal during the Chevauchée de St Michel. It is thought that the Chevauchée, or cavalcade, may have its roots in pre-Christian times, though it was later organised by the Court of the Fief of St Michel. This was the largest church held fief in the island and an offshoot of the Abbaye of St Michel in Normandy.

Winter sun at La Table des Pions

It was usually held in June, just before Corpus Christi. The idea behind it was to check that the roads were in good order, so that the processions of the Blessed Sacrament could move around unimpeded during the following week. To achieve this, the Chevauchée had within its ranks a lance bearer who carried a lance that was 11.5ft high. It was his job to check that nothing encroached onto the roadway, and see that overhanging trees came no lower than his lance. The Pions, who were dressed and equipped identically, were chosen for their good looks. At various points along the route, they were relieved of their duties, and were allowed to kiss any woman that they fancied. The only proviso was that only one Pion could kiss the same woman.

The Chevauchée disappeared when Calvinism took hold in the 16th century. It was revived again in 1813 and the last one took place on 31 May 1837. Since then, it has been re-enacted once, in 1966 for the anniversary of the Battle of Hastings.

Nearby is a fortification, Le Château de Pezeries. Though based on an earlier defensive site, what we see at present is principally Napoleonic. Follow the road north. The sight of Fort Grey in the near distance and the island of Lihou at the far end of the bay confirms that we've reached the west coast. Walk on along this beachside road until we get to the slipway at Portelet Harbour.

PORTELET SLIPWAY

Distance: 2 Miles

Bus Number: 7/7a

Toilets: Yes

Car Parking: Yes

Food: Kiosk, Hotel

Fishing boat at low tide, Fort Grey, Rocquaine

PORTELET SLIPWAY, PLEINMONT

Continue on along the coast road, passing the Imperial Hotel, as we make our way towards Fort Grey, or the Cup and Saucer as it is known. For the next mile or two we shall be walking at the side of a busy road, so be careful and make sure you can be seen.

We soon pass Fort Grey Shipwreck Museum. After the rugged cliffs of the south coast, the rest of our journey around Guernsey is delightfully flat.

1. Fort Grey

Here is a Napoleonic fortification built on the site of an earlier defence. How long the previous fortification, Le Château de Rocquaine, stood here is uncertain. The earliest record that we have is a survey undertaken in May 1680 by the Lieutenant Governor, Colonel George Legge, which mentions the fort. The soldier who inspected it, Captain Richard Leake – Master Gunner of England, said that Rocquaine Castle had: "An iron saker, this should be augmented with three 12 pounders. The fishermen say that many vessels shelter here in fowle weather".

In 1803, the Commanding Officer of the Royal Engineers, Lieutenant Colonel Mackelcan, said that the old fort should be demolished and a new defensive position built. And indeed it was: a semi circular battery was built capable of housing 12 to 14 guns. In 1804 a Martello tower was built in the centre of the redoubt and in 1809 another powder magazine was built, this time within the walls.

Today, Fort Grey is a museum dedicated to the many ships that have been lost on Guernsey's rocky coastline. Inside there are artefacts and information ranging from the wreck of HMS Sprightly that hit the Hanois reef in 1777, to the grounding of the Vermontborg on the La Capelle reef in 2003.

In common with most shallow sandy beaches around all the Channel Islands, we find a proliferation of Napoleonic and Second World War defences peppering this side of the island. Walk on and enjoy the far reaching views across Rocquaine Bay to the island of Lihou.

L'ERÉE

Distance: 2.5 Miles

Bus Number: 5/5a, 7/7a

Toilets: Yes

Car Parking: Yes

Food: Café, Restaurant, Hotel

L'ERÉE

We are able to get on a path that runs next to the beach after passing the tarmac car park which lies opposite the junction. After going past a small lay by with Bus Only painted on the road, take the road that bends left. There is a Second World War bunker just on the left. Carry straight on through a small crossroads and up a slight hill.

On the right is the ancient Le Creux és Faies Passage Tomb. Follow the road, bearing to the left, taking you to Lihou headland, with the memorial to the 18 sailors who lost their lives when the Prosperity sank in 1974. Also here is the causeway to Lihou Island.

1. Lihou Island and L'Erée Headland Ramsar Site

This 426 hectare Ramsar site, Guernsey's first, was designated on 1st March 2006. The site covers most of this corner of the island, as it includes Lihou Island, La Claire Mare and Colin Best Nature Reserves, the Shingle Bank and the outlying rocks and reefs.

Despite its small size, this site offers a large number of different habitats: vegetated shingle banks, saline lagoon, salt marsh, reed bed, three different types of seashore and the intertidal zone.

The area is especially important for birdlife. Lihou has the largest Great Black-backed Gull colony in the island. Among

the birds that breed at the nature reserves are Reed Warblers, Common Shelducks, Stonechats and Common Moorhen.

On the L'Erée Headland, expect to see Short-toed Treecreepers, Blackcaps, Common Bullfinches, and Goldcrests.

Every year, these species are joined by hundreds of migratory birds.

Retrace your steps, ignoring the turning on the right from which you came, heading downhill back to the coast road. You will notice a German tower, which is unusual in that it is built on top of a much older fortification, and is on private property. When we get to the road, walk beside the shingle bank.

The coast road bends to the right as we approach Perelle Bay. On this corner is Le Trépied Tomb dating back to circa 3-2500BC, although you will need to cross the road to see this. Continue on, and half way along the bay road we find the Perelle Battery, an emplacement for two cannon. The road bends right, leaves the beach, and heads inland. Above us is Fort Richmond. Take the second lane on the left, immediately after a phone box on the other side of the road. In a little while we meet the sea wall again, and Vazon Bay lies before us. Follow the road on the right.

Causeway view towards Lihou

VAZON BAY (SOUTH)/ RICHMOND KIOSK

After the second pebble car park, bear left up some steps to access a small promenade that runs above the beach and away from the traffic. In a few yards, bear slightly left to get on to another promenade. Go down the steps on the right by the tower, then turn left and continue on the roadside.

VAZON BAY CAFE (NORTH)

As soon as we leave the Café, carry on alongside the sea wall, don't follow the road. Walk along the path through the car park, and climb the steps to pass a restored artillery piece below us, on our left. Head towards Fort Hommet – the fortification on the headland. Go around the Martello Tower, built in 1804, staying on the left hand side, beside the beach, as we return. Cross Second World War gun emplacements set into the bank above the beach, then turn left onto a well surfaced coastal path. Before we reach the coast road again, we pass the foundations of two square buildings, which are the remains of the Albecq Medieval Settlement. When the path rejoins the road, bear left towards Cobo Bay, and carry on along the pavement. As we arrive at Cobo, we see a very tall rocky outcrop on the far side of the road with a small building on top. This is Le Guet watch tower, one of a series that ringed the coast during the Napoleonic period, which was also used during the German Occupation (if you cross the road, there is a path taking you up to the watch tower which gives wonderful views).

COBO

Pick up the path again behind the kiosk. As we approach the Rockmount public house, cross over to the pavement on the far side of the road for safety. In due course return back to the beach side of the road when another pavement appears. After a car park on the sea side of the road, the path rises through marram grass as we make for the point at Les Grandes Rocques with its fortification.

COBO

Distance: 1 Mile

Bus Number: 3/3a, 7/7a, 2

Toilets: Yes

Car Parking: Yes

Food: Kiosk, Hotel, Public House, Chip Shop, Tearoom, Restaurant

VAZON BAY CAFE (NORTH)

Distance: 1 Mile

Bus Number: 3/3a, 7/7a

Toilets: Yes

Car Parking: Yes

Food: Café, Restaurant

LES GRANDES ROCQUES

Distance: 0.5 Miles

Bus Number: 3/3a, 7/7a

Toilets: Yes

Car Parking: Yes

Food: Kiosk, Pub, Hotel

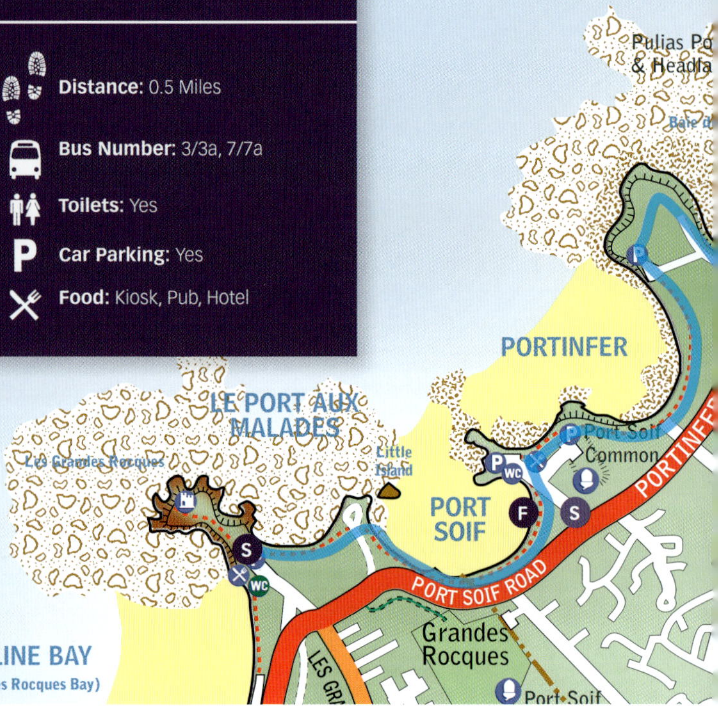

LES GRANDES ROCQUES

We pass a gravel car park as we go towards the fort. Bear left as we approach, so as to skirt the headland in a clockwise direction. As we return inland, choose the left fork and follow the path along the seashore as it goes towards the sandy haven of Port Soif. At the next small car park, turn right then bear left to reach the gravel coastal path. On reaching the car park and kiosk at the far end of the bay, we go behind the kiosk to rejoin the path.

PORT SOIF

Follow the coastal path to Portinfer and stay on the path to pass the clay pigeon range. The bits of orange clay on the ground are the remains of 'pigeons' that didn't make it! Where the path ends, we meet a tarmac lane, turn left here. Just before reaching the road, fork to the left and use the pedestrian and cycle route that runs on a bank between the road and the beach. Follow the path past a car park, and continue on up a gentle rise to pass Pulias Pond on the right. The coastal path comes out in a gravel car park, which leads to another one via a rough gravel track which continues on to the road. Here, cross over onto the pavement, turn left and walk on for about 25 metres. By the bus stop, cross the road again to reach the gravel car park, and rejoin the coastal path. It circles a wide peninsular with a number of houses below us to the right, and a loop-holed Tower at the apex. This is Rousse Tower.

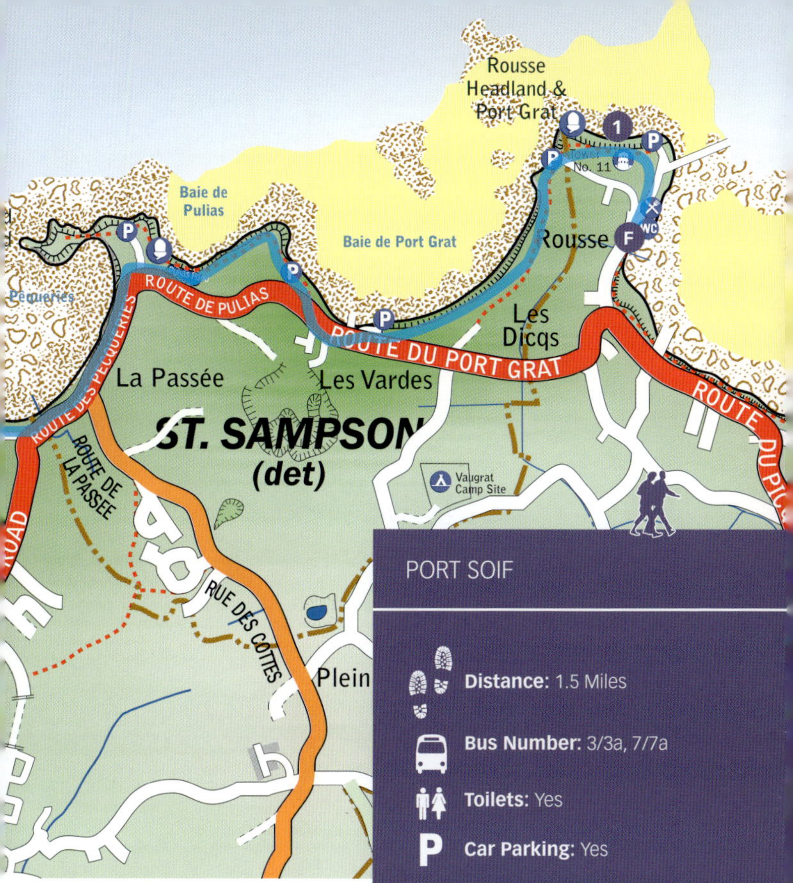

PORT SOIF

Distance: 1.5 Miles

Bus Number: 3/3a, 7/7a

Toilets: Yes

Car Parking: Yes

Food: Kiosk

1. Rousse Tower

This is tower number 11 of the 15 commissioned to protect Guernsey's coastline. It was built between 1778 and 1779, and replaces an earlier tower which stood closer to the beach. It faces Chouet Tower situated across the bay on the opposite headland and, between them, they seal off the natural harbour of Grand Havre. This tower is unique in that it has a semi-circular earth bulwark at its base, backed by a wall which runs out from either side of the tower.

This Tower was the first 18th century sea defence restored by the then Heritage Committee and Tourist Board in 1994. It followed an archaeological excavation that took place in 1993, which revealed gun platforms on the southern side of the Tower. In between these platforms were cobbles made from Purbeck stone brought in from Dorset.

The excavations also brought to light Bronze Age pottery and flint tools in the earth walls of the bulwark, which suggested that the surrounding area must have been a site of some importance. In fact, further excavations to the northwest of the tower unearthed more pottery and fragments of polished stone axes.

Continue along the path to pass the tower on the sea side, then go through a car park and pick up the coastal path again on the left.

ROUSSE

Bear left through the boat store and car park and carry on along the coastal path. We come to a track on the left and a footpath – ignore this track and proceed straight ahead on the pedestrian and cycle path which runs beside the road. When the road bends away to the right, the path carries on to pass a housing estate below us on the right. When we approach the road, fork to the left to pass a lifebuoy station and follow a rough path that runs parallel to the beach, across the grass. Make for the kiosk and car park in the distance. Across the road here is Vale Pond with observation hide. Continue past the kiosk and through the car park (the church on your right is Vale Church). Follow the coastal path on the left towards Les Amarreurs Harbour and Ladies Bay.

1. Vale Church

It is thought that a priory or chapel stood on this site as long ago as the 7th or 8th century. This is quite possible, as St Sampson brought Christianity to Guernsey sometime during the 6th century. Known as St Michel du Valle, we believe that the priory here was granted to the Benedictine monks from the Abbey of St Michel in Normandy by Duke Robert the First of Normandy.

Like many priories that had a French mother house, St Michel du Valle was seized in 1413 by King Henry V during the Suppression of the Alien Priories. Quite understandably, King Henry was unhappy that English money, given to the church as tithes and endowments, was making its way to his enemy the French.

The last remains of the priory were demolished in 1928.

Until 1806, when Sir John Doyle filled in the Braye du Valle, a narrow channel that ran from Grand Havre to what is now St Sampson's Harbour, the church stood on an island called the Clos du Valle. This island measured 1.5 miles by 2 miles, and became cut off from mainland Guernsey twice a day at high tide. In those days you had to hire a boat to take you to church. Look out for the mooring rings on the side of the church, though it is also thought that there were stepping stones or a bridge that you could use. There still is a road nearby called Pont St Michel.

A glance out to sea shows that we are directly opposite Rousse Tower and therefore approaching the other corner of Grand Havre Bay. (Here you can take a little detour and visit Les Fouaillages Burial Mound, dating back to circa 4500BC.) Walk through both the car parks ahead and beyond them we will find the coastal path between the golf course and the beach. Here, make sure that you stay to the left of the white line and also take note of the sign saying BEWARE OF STRAY GOLF BALLS.

Proceed on until we reach a rough gravel car park with Chouet Kiosk and Tearoom.

View across Colin McCathie Nature Reserve towards Vale Parish Church

ROUSSE

Distance: 1.5 Miles

Bus Number: 7/7a

Toilets: Yes

Car Parking: Yes

Food: Kiosk, Hotel, Pub

CHOUET

Distance: 0.5 Miles

Bus Number: 6/6a, 7/7a (seasonal). Walk from main road

Toilets: Yes

Car Parking: Yes

Food: Kiosk, Café

CHOUET

Leave the car park by crossing the road and turn right to walk along the gravel path alongside. Turn left onto a path, taking you towards the high ground in front of you (be careful of the golf green). As you come to the top of the hill you will notice a Second World War bunker complex, built during the German occupation of the island (1940 –1945). The bunker was part of the Flak Batterie Dolmen, an anti-aircraft defence including gun emplacements, a command bunker and a radar position. You will see the Millennium Stone ahead of you, erected to mark the year 2000. To the left of this is La Varde Passage Grave, an ancient chambered tomb and the largest megalithic structure in Guernsey. You will not fail to notice the wonderful views from here.

Continue eastwards, heading down the path towards the main road (La Jaonneuse Road). Cross the road, turning left towards the beach, car park, kiosk and café. Walk next to the sea wall, passing the front of the café, and continue on through the next car park. Looking back as we leave Pembroke Bay, you will notice the Second World War anti-tank wall.

La Varde Passage Grave

L'ANCRESSE BAY

Distance: 3.5 Miles

Bus Number: 6/6a, 7/7a (seasonal)

Toilets: Yes

Car Parking: Yes

Food: Kiosks, Restaurant, Café

L'ANCRESSE BAY

Once at the far end of the second car park, stay beside the wall and remain on the pebble strewn path that lies between the golf course and the beach. Pass the kiosk and the car park at the L'Ancresse end of the bay, and before long we should see the coastal path again, as it heads towards another tower. Make your way towards the guardhouse in the distance. Soon we get to another car park which has a huge lump of Second World War reinforced concrete in it. Walk across to regain the path on the other side. Look out for the sign saying BEWARE RIFLE RANGE COASTAL PATH DIVERSION ON THE RIGHT.

Continue along the path towards the headland. When the path forks, bear right up the incline, heading towards the next tower. We can see the rifle range on our left, which uses Fort Le Marchant as the back stop. Cross another car park and pick up the coastal path. The path bends to the right, away from the rifle range, and we see the rocky shore of Fontenelle Bay ahead.

We now find Fort Doyle at the headland, built in the mid-19th century, to protect the north approaches of St Peter Port with three heavy guns. Out to sea is the Platte Fougère Lighthouse.

1. The Platte Fougère Lighthouse

This lighthouse was built in 1909 to keep shipping away from the Brayes Reef. It was first lit on 15th March 1910, and it has the distinction of being the first unmanned lighthouse ever built. It runs automatically; the power is run out by cable from Fort Doyle.

The path turns left and we walk in the lee of a shingle bank. Carry straight on, missing two paths on the right. The path becomes wider and rough, we pass a small memorial on the left. Walk through the car park at Fort Doyle and rejoin the coastal path to the right hand side of the white house. The path then bears right and onto a gravel track.

Two tarmac roads lead away from us – take the road on the left towards a NO ENTRY sign. We follow this lane to a crossroads, turn right and then left just a few yards later. The lane curves to the right. At the next tiny crossroads, turn left, onto a lane that is part of a cycle route. The lane meanders right and left, before reaching a T junction, where we turn left.

Tower No 5, L'Ancresse Bay

View across the Little Russel to Herm, Jethou and Sark, including the Brehon Tower and Vivian Beacon

The lane makes a sweeping hairpin right; avoid the path on the left and continue following the lane. The road bends left and begins to rise. When the lane levels out, we get a good view of the islands of Herm and Jethou, as well as Brehon Tower away to the left, and Vale Castle ahead.

Brehon Tower

Built between 1854 and 1856 on the Brehon Rock, in the middle of the Little Russel between Guernsey and Herm, the Tower was constructed by Thomas Charles Du Putron from Herm granite at a cost of £8,098.

The Tower is actually elliptical in shape rather than round. When it was finished it had five 18 pound guns mounted on top, and became home to 35 artillerymen.

Like the breakwaters at St Catherine in Jersey and Braye Harbour in Alderney, the tower was built in response to the programme of fortification that Napoleon was carrying out on the nearby ports of Cherbourg, Granville and St Malo. Towards the latter part of the 19th century, when Britain and France had settled their differences, the guns were removed from the Tower.

In 1914, ownership of the tower passed into the hands of the States of Guernsey.

During the Second World War, the occupying forces mounted an anti-aircraft gun on Brehon Tower. The gun crew shot down several planes, including one of their own, a Focke-Wulfe FW190.

At the T junction at the end of this Ruette Tranquille, turn left (if you turn right here it will take you to Le Dehus Passage Tomb) and descend, then turn left again to head in the direction of the sea.

At the next corner, bear left and eventually the tarmac lane peters out onto a gravel track. Turn right, walking along the track as it runs parallel to the shore line. At the end of the track bear to the left hand side of the mound ahead to rejoin the coastal path. Here you will see the tiny island of Houmet Paradis, which is off limits from January to August due to breeding birds.

If crossing to the island, please use extreme care due to the very strong tidal currents. Continue following the path as it goes around the sheltered anchorage of Bordeaux Harbour.

When the path finishes, turn left onto the grassy area beside the road. At the far corner, turn left towards the sea and walk along the roadside for a while.

Bordeaux Harbour

St Sampson's Marina

BORDEAUX HARBOUR

We meet the coastal path again on the grass just beyond the slipway. Ahead, looms Vale Castle.

1. Vale Castle

Vale Castle was considered to be a castle of refuge for the inhabitants of the Clos du Valle which, until 1806, was a small island that was separated by a narrow stretch of water from mainland Guernsey.

The castle is built on the site of an Iron Age hill fort that dates from around 600BC. What we can see now is principally 15th century, though the entrance could be 16th or 17th century. In the 18th century, barracks were built in the courtyard. These were used for housing in the inter-war period and they were finally demolished by the Germans during 1945. It is still possible to make out the position of the barracks from the stretches of cobblestones that remain in the courtyard. Like most other defensive positions it also has fortifications which date from the Second World War.

In 1799, a number of Russian troops were billeted here. They had been fighting with the British in the Netherlands, and because the Baltic Sea was frozen over, they were unable to return home. Unfortunately, the Bill of Rights law prevented foreign troops from staying in England, so they were sent to Guernsey and Jersey for the duration. At the time Guernsey had about 6,000 Russian troops on the island who were billeted at Delancey, L'Ancresse and at Vale Castle. Several hundred of them fell ill with a fever that they had contracted while fighting on the Dutch Marshes, and many of those who died were buried on the hillside below the castle.

Back on the path again, we pass beneath the castle and the busy port of St Sampson's lies in front of us.

2. St Sampson's

This area is named after the Celtic saint who is reported to have introduced Christianity to Guernsey in the 6th century. It is said that both St Sampson and St Brelade were trained in Wales under St Illtud, and that they travelled and worked together. This can be endorsed by the fact that the churches dedicated to them, here at St Sampson's in Guernsey and at St Brelade's in Jersey, are both on beachside sites and also resemble each other quite closely. In addition both churches predate the Norman churches which form the basis for most island parish churches.

St Sampson's is a relatively young town, dating from the early years of the 19th century, when the narrow channel that ran from Grand Havre to St Sampson's was drained and filled in. Because of this, there are only three buildings of any antiquity found here: the 12th century church, Vale Castle and Le Mont Crevelt, a Napoleonic fortification on the south side of the harbour.

At the heart of St Sampson's, and the

BORDEAUX HARBOUR

Distance: 2 Miles

Bus Number: 6/6a, 7/7a (seasonal)

Toilets: Yes

Car Parking: Yes

Food: Kiosk

reason it has grown, is the harbour. In the early days the principal export was stone. Before the quays were built, boats would ground themselves on the beach and stone would be brought out by cart and tipped into the hold. The first quay was built in 1820 but as the demand for stone increased, it proved inadequate. One of the reasons for the popularity of Guernsey stone was the recent invention of McAdam's revolutionary road surface. This created an insatiable demand for the gabbro quarried nearby, because it was considered excellent for road works. The export of stone continued until the First World War, when 400,000 tons of stone were being exported annually.

The harbour we see today is the product of a number of improvements carried out between 1860 and 1880. Since the 1960s, St Sampson's has been the main port for receiving bulk cargoes such as oil, timber and coal, while St Peter Port handles passengers, containers and pleasure craft. In recent years much of the harbour has become a marina.

Carry straight on to pass a tall tower on our right. As we make our way around the three sides of the harbour, our target is the silos in the distance. Once past the clock tower, carefully cross the road to the far pavement. Continue in the direction of the silos ahead, and when the pavement finishes on the bend, use great care to cross the road. Press on through the midst of this busy port.

Very soon, we shall see our goal, St Peter Port, on the horizon. Continuing on we reach The Halfway with toilets and café across the road.

BELLE GREVE BAY

Distance: 1.5 Miles

Bus Number: 6/6a, 7/7a, 8/8a

Toilets: Yes

Car Parking: Yes

Food: Café

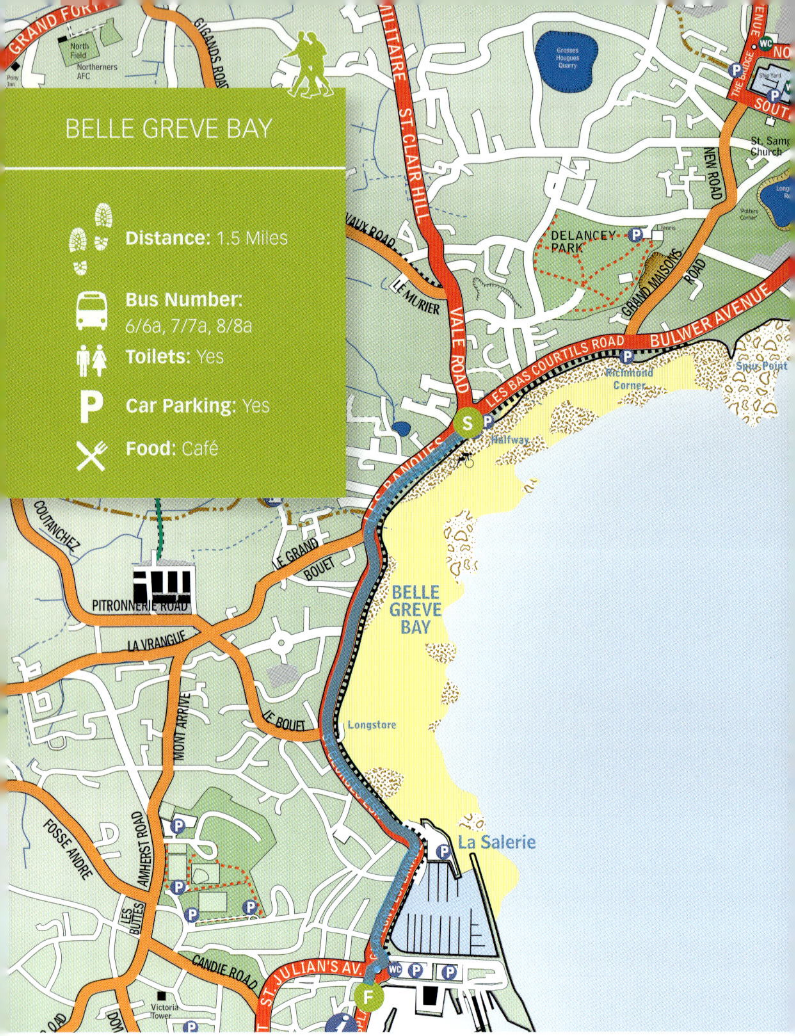

BELLE GREVE BAY

Following the coastline of this large sweeping bay, we have wonderful views of the islands of Herm, Jethou, Brecqhou and Sark. After passing the former tram sheds, home to steam and then electric trams in the 19th and early 20th century, we see some ultra modern apartments and offices. Head towards La Salerie Corner, where there is an old mooring. From here we can see that it is only a short walk before we reach the finish point. As we near the roundabout, home to the cross trees mast – which is modelled on the mizzen mast of a Napoleonic warship – bear left to stay on the pathway as it rises. Cross the road ahead carefully and follow the paved walkway, then bear right and reach our journey's end, the Liberation Monument, built in 1995 to mark 50 years of liberation from German occupation.

View towards Fort Chateau A L'Etoc

Section 3 - **ALDERNEY**

Alderney has some of the most dramatic cliff paths in the islands and, when mixed with its military history and the abundance of wildlife, it becomes an essential component of the Channel Island Way. As with the other islands, it is wise to carry a mobile phone and water, and to be aware of the incoming tide. In addition, it is advisable that young children and dogs are kept under control, particularly on cliff side paths.

Some useful phone numbers

The dialling code for Alderney is 01481.

Alderney Visitor Information Centre: 823737
Alderney Wildlife Trust: 822935
Weather Forecast: 822620
Police: 824999

In an emergency dial 112 or 999

These suggested stops are roughly two to three miles apart to make planning your walk easy. Most have car parking and toilet facilities. There are usually cafés, public houses or restaurants open nearby, but again check before setting out.

Suggested stops

1 ST ANNE
Car Parking, Public Toilets, Café Restaurant, Pubs

2 THE HARBOUR
Public Toilets, Café, Restaurant, Pubs

3 THE CAMPSITE
Car Parking, Public Toilets, Kiosk

4 LONGIS BAY
Car Parking, Public Toilets, Restaurant

ALDERNEY, AROUND ISLAND WALK

Distance: 11.5 Miles

ST ANNE

Leave the Alderney Tourism Information Centre and Wildlife Trust, turn right and make your way up Victoria Street. At the junction at the top turn left and then almost immediately right into Venelle Sauchet. At the end of this short lane, turn left, then first right into La Brecque Philippe. Walk up this road and at the

crossroads with Chemin du Meunier, continue straight on.

The tarmac gives way to cement, and soon becomes a rough farm track that leads us, through fields, towards the cliffs. When we reach the grassy cliff path, turn right. The bank on the right is the ancient barrier that kept livestock away from the crops grown on the Blaye. Until the Second World War all the land inside this hedge was cultivated in an Anglo Saxon strip farming system, reminiscent of English agriculture before the Enclosures Act.

As the path drops away, we pass a spring that feeds a small cattle trough on the right. The path rises, passes a recently rebuilt property, Les Quatre Vents, and soon arrives at the Countryside

Grazing horse near Mannez Garenne

South coast countryside

Quesnard Lighthouse

Interpretation Centre. Housed inside a wartime bunker, the centre is beneath our feet for a few yards, before a path on the right takes us to the entrance.

1. The Alderney Wildlife Trust Countryside Interpretation Centre

The Centre is housed in a Luftwaffe radio station which has been refitted to show displays of both wildlife and military history. The Centre is open throughout the year.

The Trust was started in May 2002 to promote the protection and conservation of Alderney's marine and terrestrial habitats. It is a non-profit organisation and is one of 47 Wildlife Trusts found in the United Kingdom. Despite this alliance, it is entirely self-funded, relying on its own earnings, donations and the support of its members.

For a small island, Alderney has an abundance of wildlife and a very diverse range of habitats.

In its care the Trust has two nature reserves, one at Longis, on the east of the island and one at Val du Saou, which is on the south. In addition to these, it is also responsible for a Ramsar site which lies on the island's western seaboard.

The Longis Nature Reserve covers 105 hectares, and contains 13 different habitats. They range from marine to coastal heathland and from scrub woodland to freshwater ponds, and the site is important for migrating birds.

The Val du Saou Nature Reserve also offers a temporary respite to migrating birds. This seven hectare site is mainly cliff top woodland and is home to the island's only reptile, the slow worm.

The Ramsar site – an area of internationally important wetland – has within its 1,500 hectares a varied mix of habitats. Here, the Trust is conducting a number of studies on the seabird population.

Leave the Centre and walk on. We descend into a wooded valley which is part of the Val du Saou Nature Reserve and, avoiding paths on both sides, cross the stream and climb the gravel path ahead. At the top, go towards an upright stone in the distance. Once there, take the path on the extreme left that is marked by white stones, and which goes towards the sea. Follow the path down, keeping left at any junctions. We go over a small bridge.

The views from this path are exceptional; look out for signs of quarrying in the cliff side below us. During late spring, at the mouth of one of these quarries, the national rare spotted rock rose can be seen carpeting the edge of the path.

2. Quarrying

The quarries here are probably pre-Victorian, as many smaller ones would have been dug to source stone close to the building site. There was a huge demand for stone once the British Government started fortifying Alderney. When the commercial jetty at Braye was built at the end of the 19th century, export became possible and Alderney stone was popular for road making. In addition to this jetty, a pier was built at La Cachaliere, on the island's south coast, to service the quarry that opened there in the 1900s. The industry was at its height just before the Second World War, and by that time about 20% of the working population was employed in the quarries. The largest employer was the Channel Islands Granite Company Limited. This owned or leased nearly 700 acres and employed around 100 men. Before the Second World War, there were quarries at Mannez, Battery Quarry and York Hill. Work at La Cachaliere stopped following the loss of the steamer Tyne, which sank nearby after loading stone at the pier.

After the war, Mannez Quarry remained in use, supplying stone for the repair of the breakwater.

The path returns inland and meets another. Turn left here and carry on southwards towards the Couriaux Headland. We head inland, eventually reaching a rough tarmac track. Turn left and follow it downhill; at the bottom there is a small spring-fed pond. Just beyond and behind the tall bank is the site of Lager Sylt, a concentration camp which was eventually run by the SS. Still visible in front of the bank are the foundations of the camp commandant's chalet. During the war a tunnel led through the bank into the camp so that the commandant had easy access.

Walk on along the track. The gate pillars of the camp, which bear a memorial plaque to those who lost their lives during the war, can still be seen over on the right. Once past the gates, turn left into the gorse. Bear right along an avenue that cuts straight through the bushes, and which emerges in a grassy area. Here follow the wide path that curves right towards some stones. The track winds its way near the Telegraph Tower and away again.

3. The Telegraph Tower

Built around 1809 on Beacon Heights, this tower could communicate with Guernsey and Jersey by means of a repeating telegraph on Sark using the Mulgrave semaphore system. It was built at a time when the island felt under threat from the French, as hostilities had resumed in 1803.

Peter Archer Mulgrave, who had invented this revolutionary means of signalling, later went into the Colonial Service, and was sent to Van Diemens Land in Australia as Superintendant of Schools. Here he established the Tamar Valley semaphore telegraph, which sent messages from Georgetown to Launceston, a distance of nearly 30 miles.

The track dips and rises, and bends right. Below us is Telegraph Bay – unfortunately access to the bay from onshore is now impossible due to erosion. Head towards the bench, then turn right to descend to a white stone marker below. At the marker turn left, and descend a shallow valley that falls away to the right between the brambles. Follow the track as it continues downhill. When the path levels out, heading southwest towards the sea, it narrows and goes along the top of a bank for a short distance. Ahead are Les Etacs, and thousands of Gannets.

4. Les Etacs

Les Etacs, or the Garden Rocks, and Ortac which lies farther out in the Swinge, are home to a population of around 7,000 breeding pairs of Northern Gannets. These, the most southern colonies of these birds, represent over 3% of the world's Northern Gannet population.

The Gannets began nesting on Les Etacs in 1939. They winter in Atlantic waters off the coast of Africa and arrive here in the spring. Their breeding period is from March to September, which means that Gannets stay in Alderney a lot longer than many other sea birds. They incubate their eggs for more than six weeks and, once hatched, the chick remains in the nest for over two months. Gannets stay in pairs for several years.

The Gannet is by far the largest sea bird found around our shores. Their wing span is around six feet and they weigh eight or nine pounds. They principally feed on fish such as mackerel, sand eels and herring, and the sight of them diving, with their wings swept back into a W shape is impressive. They can dive from a height of 40 metres, and can reach depths of up to 30 metres below the surface. Their speed of entry into the water can be more than 60mph.

Gannets are known to live to nearly 30 years of age, although some as old as 37 have been recorded.

Well before the cliff edge, turn right and climb the path that rises very steeply ahead. At the top, bear right and head towards the Ramsar site interpretation board and the bench. Walking inland, we come across the first artillery emplacement of Batterie Annes. On meeting a wide track, turn left and follow it as it passes the other emplacements. The track meets another one near what looks like a bridge, although there is no stream or ravine beneath it. Here, turn left along a rough track and return to the cliffs.

5. Batterie Annes

Here, on the Giffoine, is one of the five coastal batteries that the Germans built during the Occupation. It was made up of four 15 cm SK C/28 guns that had a

South coast cliffs

Books for sale
High Street, St Anne

range of 13 miles, and was manned by a naval artillery unit. The guns themselves were turreted and mounted in open pits and the bunkers underneath them were for the gun crews that were on duty, while beside each gun is a bunker for the off-duty gun crew. In common with other batteries on Alderney, this site was self-contained; it had a generator for electricity, its own water supply, an armoury, a workshop, stores and canteen. It also had the most modern guns of all the island's batteries.

Batterie Annes is one of three medium coastal artillery batteries built in Alderney. The others were Batterie Elsass, with three 17 cm SK L/40 guns, which was at Fort Albert, and Batterie Blucher, housing four 15 cm K18 guns in open pits on high ground to the east of St Anne. All three batteries were eventually controlled by a MP3 direction-finding tower on the Mannez Garenne Hill, now known as the Odeon.

Batterie Blucher was manned by an army unit and the other two batteries by sailors from the Marineartillerieabteilung or MAA 605, whose headquarters were at Fort Albert.

We arrive in a wide grassy area which allows us fabulous views of both Les Etacs and Fort Clonque. A narrow path on the right that goes through the gorse, leads us down towards the fort. Keep left when the path divides, to pass a wide channel cut into the cliff on our right. This was the site of a German search light that ran on rails inside the channel. At the cliff side end of the channel is a carpet of Hottentot fig; this is not a native of the island, but rather a plant that has been brought here, and which is massively invasive.

From this vantage point, on a clear day, we should be able to see the Casquets reef about seven miles offshore.

6. The Casquets

This notorious reef lies seven miles west of Alderney and very close to the Channel shipping lanes. It has been the cause of numerous wrecks, notable among which was the 100 gun, HMS Victory, flagship of Admiral Sir John Balchen, that sank in 1744, with the loss of 1,000 lives, and the SS Stella, that sank in thick fog in 1899, with the loss of 102 lives.

Trinity House granted Thomas Le Cocq a patent to erect a lighthouse in 1723. In order to distinguish it from French and English lighthouses, three lights set in a horizontal triangle were proposed. These held coal fires burning within a glazed framework. The lights were named St Peter, St Thomas and Dungeon, and were first lit in October 1724.

The lighthouses came back into Trinity House ownership in 1785, when Thomas Le Cocq's lease expired. In 1818, a revolving mechanism was fitted to each light, and each was raised by 30 feet in 1854.

During the 19th century, the keeper, a Mr Houguez and his entire family lived on Les Casquets for 18 years. They even grew their own vegetables on a small patch of soil, which is still visible today. They were immortalised by the poet Algernon Charles Swinburne in his poem Les Casquets:

Hardly the breadth of a few brief paces,
Hardly the length of a strong man's stride,
The small court flower lit with children's faces
Scarce held scope for a bud to hide.

Yet here was a man's brood reared and hidden
Between the rocks and the towers and the foam,
Where peril and pity and peace were bidden
As guests to the same sure home.

Today all the towers are still in use, although it is only St Peter's tower that shows a light. Standing 120 feet above sea level, it has an intensity of 452,000 candela and a range of 24 nautical miles. The east tower, Dungeon, houses the fog signalling equipment, while inside St Thomas' tower is the generator, with a helipad on top.

Part of the Gannet colony at Les Etacs
©Joanna Parmentier

Crab Pots. Inner Harbour, Alderney

Since November 1990, the lighthouse has run automatically. It is monitored by Trinity House at Harwich.

The path wends its way down into a valley, and about halfway down, it bends right and runs parallel to the valley side. Walk across a dry stone wall and climb for a few yards, then turn left towards the sea. Look out for a steep narrow path that goes off on the right, and climb it to regain a wider path that passes the walkers' shelter which is in a bunker to the side of the track.

Once past the shelter, bear left down a wide track which zig-zags its way towards the beach. At the bottom, carry on along the track towards the silhouette of Fort Tourgis in the distance. We cross a bridge spanning a natural stream bed that runs onto the beach. The island offshore is Burhou.

7. Burhou

Burhou is a small island half a mile long and 400 yards wide that sits in the fast flowing waters of the Swinge. A cottage was built here during the early 19th century as a shelter for ship-wrecked sailors, on the instructions of General John Le Mesurier, the governor of Alderney. In the 1900s a French couple lived there, with a small menagerie of pigs and goats. During the German Occupation, the cottage was shelled by the German gun batteries ashore and only the walls remained. The States of Alderney erected a hut there in 1953, which in later years has been improved, and now provides accommodation for the scientists and naturalists who visit Burhou.

The island sits almost in the middle of Alderney's Ramsar site, which stretches from just south of Les Etacs to Platte Saline Bay. The Ramsar site is twice the size of Alderney, and encompasses the islands of Les Etacs, Ortac, Burhou and the reefs of Great Nannel and Renonquet. As in the other islands, the site is sustainably managed to conserve the indigenous creatures and the habitat for future generations.

From the middle of March to the beginning of August, Burhou is a bird sanctuary which is closed to the public. The island is home to 11 species of breeding birds including Storm Petrels, Puffins, Shags, Cormorants, Razorbills, Guillemots and Lesser Black-backed Gulls. The sanctuary's most charismatic visitor, the Puffin, arrives in April. At present there are about 120 breeding pairs of Puffin on the island.

As we near Fort Tourgis, Alderney's second largest Victorian fort, the track divides and we bear left to continue along the beach-side track. We pass a wartime coastal casement which still has the wooden cladding around the gun embrasure. The wood was put there to catch any shrapnel that ricocheted off the concrete. A little further on is a granite carponnier, which offered lines of rifle fire along the fort's impressive outer walls, the Victorian answer to what we have just seen in reinforced concrete.

The road curves beneath Fort Tourgis, and meets the hill that climbs past the fort. Bear left across the sandy track towards the gravel depot; carry on past the tennis courts and the row of beach-side houses and walk straight on to go through a cutting in the bank ahead. We emerge onto a gravel path that runs beside the road. The two buildings on the right are the St John Ambulance Headquarters, and the Fire Station. Just behind them is the Mignot Memorial Hospital.

Continue on – the large building on the right is the power station that generates the island's electricity; the quarry beside it provides water to cool the plant, while the large blue tanks hold the fuel for the generators. Walk on to the crossroads, next to the filling station, then turn left and walk down to the Inner Harbour which is just on the right.

8. The Breakwater

At the beginning of the 1840s, relations between France and Britain had broken down. This, together with the French building or enlarging harbours all the way from Dunkirk to Brest, began to ring alarm bells in Parliament.

View towards Fort Chateau a L'Etoc

In fact, one of the projects nearing completion in France was the harbour and arsenal at Cherbourg, which had become a matter of concern to the Admiralty. So in 1842, it was proposed that 'Harbours of Refuge', in reality harbours to house the British Channel Fleet, be built in Jersey, Guernsey and Alderney – which, because of its proximity to Cherbourg, would also provide an ideal observation post.

Work started in 1847, and was undertaken by the civil engineering company of Jackson and Bean, which was also engaged on the breakwater at St Catherine in Jersey at the same time. Although both harbours were never finished, work at St Catherine progressed better as it did not have to withstand the Atlantic gales, fierce tides and much greater depth of water that hampered work here at Braye.

The proposed harbour, which was to have a western breakwater beginning at Grosnez Point and an eastern breakwater that started at Rozelle Point, was to enclose 67 acres. But by 1858, the harbour plans had grown, so that now the proposed western arm had more than doubled in length, and the eastern arm was to extend out from Grois Rocks by Chateau a L'Etoc. This would have increased the size of the harbour to 150 acres.

By 1864 the breakwater stretched 1,600 yards out to sea, but even then, this didn't provide a sufficient depth of water for the huge ships that the Navy were soon to have. Work stopped and the harbour was never completed.

In 1872, the final 600 yards of the wall was abandoned and it rapidly fell away, leaving a hazardous reef which still remains a danger to shipping. It was said that the breakwater had cost £1.5 million to build and maintain over its 25 year life. Today Guernsey pays to upkeep the breakwater as part of its defence contribution, and in 2008 the costs of upkeep were £456,000.

Saye Bay

Alderney: The Harbour

Toilets: Yes

Food: Café, Restaurant, Pub

Stroll around the harbour, and up the slight hill passing the Harbour Office. The road comes out on a wide concrete area, so cross carefully to the granite building ahead, which houses the RNLI. Once there, turn right and head inland, beside the beach, towards the tall buildings ahead.

Continue on between the buildings, most of which were originally warehouses that backed directly onto Braye Beach, and at the end turn left.

After a few yards we can get on the grass of Braye Common. Continue along the common and, when it finishes, walk on the verge by the crash barriers, then climb the gentle hill past the Mount Hale Battery, towards Fort Albert. At the top of the hill, turn left onto the gravel track that leads to the fort. Below are the buildings of the Arsenal. The three-sided building without a roof is a fives court. This was a game very similar to squash, played by two or four players, who used a shaped padded glove rather than a racket.

Alderney: The Campsite

Toilets: Yes

Food: Kiosk

At the top, the track swings around to the fort entrance on the right. We need to bear left, to walk beneath the ramparts, and then on to descend the narrow path, through bracken, towards the beach below. On meeting another path turn left, and carry on downhill. At the fork, continue straight on until we reach a wide beachside track. Turn right and follow the track inland. When we get to a gate on the left, go through the gate or the gap next to it, and cross the campsite to the far side.

Leaving the campsite, we should be able to see a short tunnel ahead on the left. This originally supported the railway line which supplied the stone to build Fort Chateau a L'Etoc, a Napoleonic fort built in 1855 to house 23 guns and 128 soldiers, and now supports the road. Go through the tunnel into Arch Bay, turn right and follow the sandy path which soon emerges on the roadside. At the road turn left, and walk on beside the beach. Across the road is Corblets Quarry, an abandoned quarry which now serves as a reserve water supply.

After the last bench, take a path that leaves the far end of the car park to go around Fort Corblets. The walls of the fort blend in with the rock on which it is built – in places it is hard to make out where the walls begin and the rocks end and the strata of the rocks appear to be running at an angle. At the road turn left.

As we approach Mannez Lighthouse, take the path to the left of the light, and beware of the fog horn! Out to sea is the ruined Fort Les Hommeaux Florains. At the road, turn left and make for the next fort, which is only a few yards further on. Once past Fort Quesnard, the road bends away to the right, leave it here, bear left and make your way down a wide path that goes towards the sea. This flat grassy path takes us to Longis Bay. The area from Fort Corblets around to the far side of the Bay is principally a nature reserve, and within it are Mannez Pond and Longis Pond, which we will pass shortly. The offshore fort is Fort Houmet Herbe.

In due course the track comes out in open duneland, continue along as it runs between a granite wall and a sandy mound on the left. This was a Victorian rifle range; the apparatus on the left, beneath the sandy mound, was used to raise and lower the targets, while the mound was the back stop that caught the bullets. The wall on the right was to protect a row of quarrymen's cottages, which can still be seen in the undergrowth, from stray bullets.

Walk away from the sea and up to the road. Turn left and walk on for a short distance. Look out for a path on the other side of the road that is marked by a white stone with a green stripe. Take this path and follow it inland. Where there are any junctions, go straight on. The bird hide overlooking Longis Pond can be seen over to the right. When we reach a T junction in the path, either turn right to visit the hide or turn left to carry on along our route.

Back at the road, turn right and pass the building on the left – the Nunnery. Behind it are toilets and a car park. Pass the road that leads to the toilets, climb a slight incline and take the next left. Ahead are a pair of pillars with Private Residence –

Alderney: Longis Bay

Toilets: Yes

Car Parking: Yes

Food: Restaurant

No Through Road on one of them, so go through these and climb the hill. Below us, out in the bay, is Fort Raz, while immediately beneath us, we can see the Longis Lines, a 14 gun Victorian defence position. The semi-circular metal rails with a stone and metal spigot in the middle is a gun position. The gun would pivot on the spigot, assisted by wheels that ran on the rail behind.

When we draw level with a square building on the right, walk on for a few paces and take a look behind it. Between it and a similar building is the original entrance to Essex Castle, now almost hidden from view. The hill flattens out: avoid the first path on the left but take the second wider track that bears off to the left. When we reach the field gate, continue on using the wider track that runs ahead. Over to the right is a fabulous view of the harbour, the breakwater, Braye Bay and Burhou.

Where there is a junction in the path, turn right towards the fields ahead. The path descends and narrows as it cuts through the gorse, and winds its way along the cliff side. A wider grassy path comes in from the right; here turn left and follow it downhill. As we near the waste disposal plant, turn right onto a wider well-trodden path that leads to the road. At the road, turn right and walk along it for a few yards, then turn left back onto the cliff path.

This path, which takes us back to our starting point in St Anne, is wide, grassy and an absolute delight to walk on, dipping and rising as it follows the coastline ahead. It bends right, goes between two stretches of fencing and comes to a junction with a well-used farm track. Turn left here. Pass a track that goes off on the right then the path begins to climb, and we catch sight of Les Quatre Vents ahead. It bends to the right and climbs a little further to a fork in the path. Here take the right fork and return along the farm track to St Anne.

To get back to the Alderney Tourism Information Centre and Wildlife Trust, cross over the crossroads with Chemin du Meunier into La Brecque Philippe. At the end of the street turn left, then second right into Venelle Sauchet. When this little lane meets the High Street turn left, then immediately turn right into Victoria Street.

Longis Bay

The Alderney Tourism Information Centre and Wildlife Trust are about 200 yards away on the left.

La Coupée

Section 4 - **SARK**

Although it is one of the smaller islands on the Channel Island Way, Sark offers some great walking. In fact, it is surprising how big the island becomes once you are underway. It has verdant cliffs, magnificent views and a relaxed pace of life. As with the other islands, it is wise to carry a mobile phone and water, and to be aware of the incoming tide. As many of the cliff paths are close to the edge, it is essential that young children and dogs are kept under control.

Some useful phone numbers

The dialling code for Sark is 01481.

Sark Visitor Information Centre: 832345

Sark Doctor: 832045

Sark Constable: 07781 101908

In an emergency dial 112 or 999

This is a circular route which is about ten miles long. As the route is not always on the cliff side, there are two or three detours mentioned, so walkers can visit various points of interest as they go around. These are not included in the total mileage.

Unlike the other islands much of this walk is on private land, so please follow the country code: walk at the edge of fields and always shut gates behind you.

Suggested stops

LA SABLONNERIE HOTEL
Restaurant, Tea Gardens

ISLAND HALL
Public Toilets

MASELINE HARBOUR
Public Toilets, Café

SARK,
AROUND ISLAND WALK

Distance: 10 Miles

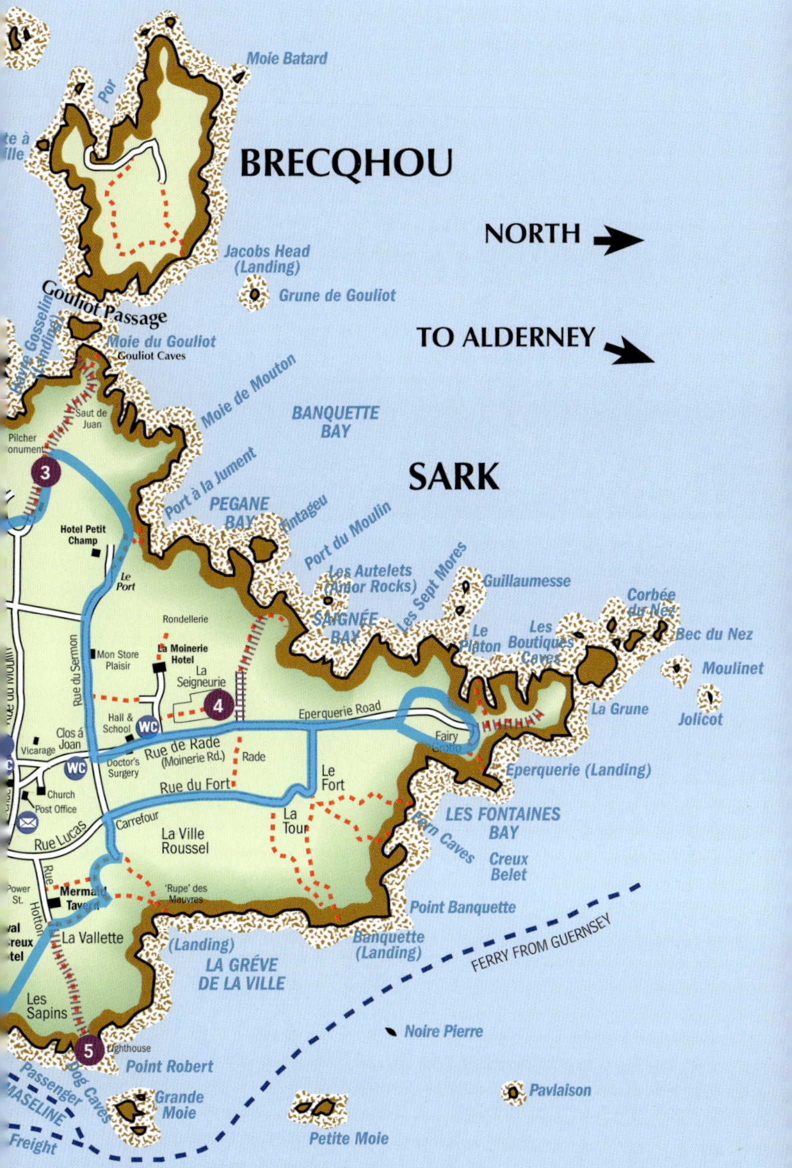
Moie Batard
BRECQHOU
NORTH
Jacobs Head (Landing)
Grune de Gouliot
Gouliot Passage
Moie du Gouliot
Gouliot Caves
TO ALDERNEY
Moie de Mouton
BANQUETTE BAY
Saut de Juan
SARK
Port à la Jument
PEGANE BAY
Tintageu
Port du Moulin
Hotel Petit Champ
Le Port
Les Autelets
Guillaumesse
Corbée du Nez
Bec du Nez
Moulinet
Jolicot
SAIGNÉE BAY
Les Sept Mores
Le Platon
Les Boutiques Caves
La Grune
Rondellerie
Mon Store Plaisir
La Moinerie Hotel
La Seigneurie
Rue du Sermon
Eperquerie Road
Fairy Grotto
Eperquerie (Landing)
Hall & School
WC
Clos á Joan
Vicarage
Rue de Rade (Moinerie Rd.)
Rade
Doctor's Surgery
Le Fort
Rue du Fort
Church
Post Office
Carrefour
La Tour
LES FONTAINES BAY
Fern Caves
Rue Lucas
La Ville Roussel
Creux Belet
Power St.
Mermaid Tavern
'Rupe' des Mauvres
Point Banquette
Rue Hotton
La Vallette
(Landing)
Banquette (Landing)
FERRY FROM GUERNSEY
LA GRÉVE DE LA VILLE
Les Sapins
Noire Pierre
Lighthouse
Point Robert
Passenger
Bog Caves
Grande Moie
Pavlaison
Petite Moie
Freight

This walk begins almost the moment you get off the boat, because our route starts just beyond the tunnel which is yards from the jetty. After passing through the tunnel, walk up the hill for about 200 yards, and take the path on the left marked Foot Path. Climb the steps. When the path splits, take the left fork to Les Laches. Climb the winding steps; a superb view of Creux Harbour lies ahead over to the left. At the top, where the path levels off into an open area, bear left and continue on the wide track that leads through the trees.

Follow the track as it bends right and heads inland. Walk on until we reach a small wooden gate beside a signpost on the left. Go through the gate and follow the finger post towards Derrible Bay and Hog's Back. Go through another gate, and then walk straight ahead towards the sea. The depression in the ground on the right is the Dew Pond, a man-made water catchment lined with clay used for watering animals. Below us is Derrible Bay. At the sign for Hogs Back, turn right and carry on, with the sea on our left. In a few yards a set of steps appears in a gap in the gorse on the left so descend these, go through a gate, and descend further. Avoid a path on the left, which leads to Derrible Hole, and continue straight on. The path rises again through the undergrowth, before reaching a T junction. Here, turn right to head back inland. (If we turn left, we go to the Hogs Back, where there is a cannon, and extensive views over Derrible and Dixcart Bays and south to Little Sark.) Walk on the right hand side of a field for a short distance, before the track bends left onto rough gravel, descends and arrives at a rough staggered crossroads.

Go over the crossroads onto concrete, follow the sign to Dixcart Bay, and continue on through the woods. When the path divides take the left fork, then left again at the next junction shortly afterwards. When we get to another path, turn left towards Dixcart Bay. The path descends beside a cottage, and after some distance goes over a small footbridge. Avoid a hairpin bend which turns up to the right and continue beside the stream as it makes its way down to the sea. At the next path uphill, bear right and climb. Dixcart Bay is on the left below us.

1. Operation Basalt

On the 3rd October 1942, at about 11.30pm, twelve commandos from the Small-Scale Raiding Force, led by Major John Geoffrey Appleyard, landed on Sark. Their brief was to gain intelligence and capture prisoners for interrogation. The raiding party landed at the Hogs Back, between Derrible and Dixcart Bays, and made their way inland toward La Jaspellerie where they expected to find German troops. At La Jaspellerie, they found the recently-widowed Mrs Frances Pittard, who answered their questions and directed them to the Dixcart Hotel. One of the commandos dispatched the sentry outside the hotel annexe, and they went in. Inside they found five Germans asleep, they captured them and left.

Once the German troops, who had their hands tied but were not gagged, realised how few commandos there were, they began to raise the alarm. In the ensuing confusion, two Germans escaped, two were shot dead and one, who was wounded, remained with the commandos. The commandos made their way back to the rendezvous, and left Sark by MTB at around 3.45am.

When Hitler discovered that the dead soldiers had been bound, he was furious, and he sent an order to shackle 1,400 troops that had been captured at Dieppe. In retaliation, Britain chained an equal number of German prisoners held in Canada. Seeing that the situation could escalate, the Swiss Government stepped in, and proposed that both sides should simultaneously unchain their prisoners. The British did so, but the German Government refused to until the British Government gave an assurance that no prisoners of war would be shackled in future.

Despite this assurance, some days later Hitler issued an order instructing his forces to kill any commandos captured in the future.

The small oak tree behind the memorial was grown from an acorn by Guernsey resident, Marco Ciotti. Rather poignantly,

Cottages on Little Sark

Carriages setting off for the day

Sark Venture leaving Maseline Bay

Cliff path to La Coupée

Mr Ciotti took his acorn from one of the oak trees at the Commonwealth War Graves at Monte Cassino in Italy where Major Appleyard's memory is honoured.

At the top, just after the small memorial to Major Appleyard, we meet a dusty track; turn left here. Immediately before an S bend, go over a stile on the left. Following the finger post to La Coupée, walk on beside a fence, towards the far left hand corner. The path runs through a tunnel of vegetation, dips and rises, and on the left we can see Dixcart Bay again. Before long, we are able to see Little Sark in front of us, with the small islet of La Breniere just to the left of it. Further out to sea, the pyramid-shaped islet is L'Etac, one of the few places that puffins come ashore to breed in spring.

Food: Hotel

The path curves to the right and climbs slightly. On meeting the road, by the Carriage Park, turn left. Cross La Coupée, the narrow isthmus between Sark and Little Sark, and proceed uphill into Little Sark. The islands on our right are Guernsey, Jethou and Herm with Brecqhou on the extreme right hand side, closest to Sark. Walk on and after some distance we reach La Sablonnerie Hotel,

La Coupée

La Sablonnerie, Little Sark

here turn left towards the Venus Pool and Port Gorey, and continue along the track as it winds its way past quaint cottages and out through the gorse. Over to the right we can see the ventilation shafts of the old silver mines.

2. The Silver Mines

Mineral exploration took place in Sark in the early 1830s. Copper, silver and lead and other minerals were found, but it was not until 1836 that a mine was sunk here at Port Gorey on Little Sark. Over 200 Cornish miners were brought in, a 120hp steam engine was installed and a narrow gauge railway was constructed.

Four shafts – Sark's Hope, Le Pelley's, Prince's and Vivian's – were sunk down to a depth of 180 metres and galleries run out, some under the sea bed. Initially the mine promised good returns but as time went on, the quality of the ore declined and the seam became narrow. Overheads to run the mine were high; coal had to be imported to run the steam engine, and once mined the ore had to be sent by sea to be smelted. At the final audit, £34,000 had been spent to raise £4,000 of ore from the ground.

One of the people most affected by this was Sark's Seigneur, Ernest Le Pelley who had become Seigneur on the death of his brother Pierre, who was drowned off the north of L'Epecquerie Common in 1839. Like his brother, Ernest Le Pelley had also invested heavily in the mining company. Eventually he went bankrupt, and was forced to mortgage the Fief to Jean Allaire, an ex-privateer and reputedly the richest man in Guernsey, to raise £4,000. Ernest Le Pelley died in 1849, and the debt passed on to his 19 year-old son and heir, Peter Carey Le Pelley. Unable to meet the interest payments, young Le Pelley was forced to hand over the Fief to Jean Allaire's daughter, Marie Collings, who called in the debt when her father died in 1852.

It is from this beginning that the present line of Seigneurs is descended.

WARNING – The whole site of the silver mines is privately owned and it is dangerous to explore it. Occasionally a few people who have signed disclaimers may be engaged in industrial archaeology on the site. All other persons must keep strictly to the paths at all times.

As some of the cliff paths on Little Sark are close to the edge it is essential that young children and dogs are kept under control.

Go through a metal gate on the right – there is sign just on the far side. Take the directions for the Venus Pool and bear left. Continue down towards the sea, avoiding a path on the right. There is a rock scramble here to Venus Pool which is not visible from the headland. When we emerge in an open area next to a bench, turn right to pursue a path that rises and returns inland among the gorse, passing alongside a wooden barrier close to the cliff edge. Look out for the derelict remains of the mine buildings hidden in the undergrowth on the left of the path. As we get near the last remaining corner of a tall engine shaft, take the second path on the left, just before the shaft, to go up some steps and then over a stile. On the far side of the valley are the ruined mine buildings, and below us is Port Gorey.

Go over another stile – the path meanders through the gorse. Avoid a path on the left that goes to Rouge Caneau, but bear right and then follow a rough bendy one up to another stile. Go over this, then turn left to walk alongside a barbed-wire fence and cross another stile. Then follow the path to the right, using care because we are close to the cliff edge. Keep to the path on the right. At the fork bear right and climb a stile immediately afterwards. Keep to the left hand side of the field until the next stile slightly to the right, where you will see a house overlooking the sea. Turn right after the stile and walk up the right hand side of the field, away from the sea. Go through the gate at the far corner at the top of the field and turn right on to a track. Carry on along the track, and follow it as it bends left, then right between some cottages, and turn left to pass the Tea Gardens and La Sablonnerie again on your right. Soon we are on the road back to La Coupée.

Return over La Coupée, and continue straight on for about half a mile. When we get to the first road on the right, which goes to Dixcart Bay, take the grassy path, a few yards further up on the opposite side of the road. Go through a gate. When this finally emerges on to a rough clearing, turn left and walk towards a lone thatched cottage. To visit the Pilcher Monument, turn left when you reach the road.

3. The Pilcher Monument

This monument is dedicated to London oil merchant, Jeremiah Pilcher, who drowned in the Gouliot Passage in 1868.

The story is typical of many sea faring tragedies in that the victims were advised not to go to sea that October evening in 1868, but they disregarded that sage advice. Pilcher, together with brothers Agnew and Walter Giffard, Russell Renouf and a Dr Gatehouse, left Sark from Havre Gosselin, bound for Guernsey.

The tide and an ever increasing wind carried them south. Their 18ft boat was found wrecked on the Contentin Peninsular, and the bodies of the Giffard brothers and Russell Renouf were washed up at different points around Sark's coast. Jeremiah Pilcher's body was found two months later on the Isle of Wight, but the body of Dr Gatehouse was never recovered.

The granite obelisk above Havre Gosselin was put up by Pilcher's widow.

To continue on our Around Island Route, at the road turn right and go straight on between farm gates, then turn immediately left, to walk under an avenue of trees with a granite wall on the right and then a barbed wire fence. Go through a metal gate and turn right to go along a grassy track. The large island close to Sark is Brecqhou, privately owned by the multi-millionaire Barclay brothers.

Here on the Gouliot Headland, we are in Sark's four hectare Ramsar site which was designated on 9th April 2007. Beneath us are the Gouliot Caves, home to a colourful and diverse array of sea anemones, sponges and sea squirts, and the first sea cave system to be incorporated into a Ramsar site in the British Isles.

When the track comes out between two benches, turn almost hairpin right and go through another gate. Keeping on the left hand side of the field, carry on to the next gate. After going through this, the track becomes much clearer.

Follow the track as it passes between a stone barn and a corrugated barn, turns right then left, and finally reaches a T junction beside a finger post – turn left here. The track dips, rises and bends right and left. The granite building on the left, Le Port a La Jument, is one of the original 40 homes that the settlers built when Sark was colonised in the 16th century. The original tenant was Nicolas du Val, whose grandson Josué sold it to Benoist Le Gros in 1666, a sale that was challenged by the Seigneur. In 1681, the property was sold to the sitting tenant, Abraham Vaudin. The house remained in Vaudin family ownership until 1938, when Mary Vaudin died unmarried. Follow the road as it bends to the right. When we arrive at another junction, bear left to pass the graveyard and the Methodist Chapel on our right. Unsurprisingly this road is called Rue du Sermon, because preachers would compose their sermons on the way to chapel.

Walk on past the sports field and, at the crossroads ahead, turn left, towards La Seigneurie, Port du Moulin, L'Eperquerie and the Medical Centre. There is a finger post at the junction. After a few yards we pass the Island Hall on our left.

Toilets: Island Hall

Further up the road we pass La Seigneurie, the official home of the head of Sark, the Seigneur.

4. La Seigneurie

Despite this fine building being called La Seigneurie, it is not the original manor

La Seigneurie

Sark signposts

La Seigneurie Gardens

house, which is situated further south on the island.

The present Seigneurie, built in 1675, was originally called La Perronerie, from Perron which means balustrade. It is one of the original 40 tenements, and the first owner was Isaac Le Gros. It became La Seigneurie in 1730, when Susanne Le Pelley, the daughter of Jean Le Gros, purchased the Fief from the executor of the will of the previous Seigneur, James Milner. Mrs Le Pelley chose to stay in her family home and Le Manoir became the Vicarage.

After Susanne Le Pelley's death in 1733, her son Nicolas Le Pelley extended the building and, exercising his Seigneurial right, put up a colombier to keep pigeons. The tower that dominates the building was erected as a signalling point to Guernsey by the Reverend William Collings in the latter half of the 19th century.

After we pass La Seigneurie, a road on the left will allow us to detour to the Window in the Rock, Port du Moulin and La Maison Rouge Art Gallery. Otherwise continue until we arrive at a bend in the road. Here walk straight on, to follow the finger post to L'Eperquerie and the Shooting Range. When the track reaches an open area, take the path on the extreme left, allowing us to make a circuit of the common.

The path descends, and curves to the right. Later on, where the path forks, keep left and walk towards the headland. Eventually we arrive beneath the corner of a dry stone wall that is high above us on the right. Here we have two choices: we can either turn left and detour to the headland, or continue around to the right and return inland. On the return route we walk beside the wall for some distance and below us to the left is L'Eperquerie Landing. Here, you can see the black cannon barrels sunk into the ground, which were used as bollards to tie up boats.

We pass one of Sark's ancient cannons, adjacent to a ruined guardhouse which was inhabited until after the Second World War. Before this, the tiny building was home to Walter and Edith Hamon, their six children and a grand-daughter! The Hamons were deported during the Occupation in February 1943. Once again, we have a choice of routes – take the path on the extreme left and follow it downhill. After the path bends left, go through the gap in the bank on the right and down some rocky steps. Below us is Fontaine Bay. At the next fork, bear right and climb the steps. At the top, where we meet a well-used track, turn left and follow the gentle slope upwards, avoiding any paths on either side. When the track has almost levelled out, it meets another track at a T junction, here turn right and soon we arrive back at the start of our circuit. Return back to the sign post for L'Eperquerie and the Shooting Range and turn left onto a road.

At the next fork, bear right. The road bends left and right, and is then followed by a long straight stretch bordered by telegraph poles. At the staggered crossroads, turn left following the finger post directions to Greve de la Ville and The Lighthouse. Turn right at the next junction, another signpost repeats the previous instructions. The road meanders past another fine granite building that was one of the original 40 homesteads. Continue on the well-used track, which bends right and runs under some pine trees. It is signposted: The Village and the Mermaid Tavern. If we take the next left, it is possible to detour to The Lighthouse on Point Robert, but note that the building is closed to the public.

5. Point Robert Lighthouse

The lighthouse was built by Trinity House in 1913, and stands over 200ft above sea level. Despite having the buildings and other structures normally associated with an onshore station, Trinity House classes this cliff side light as a rock lighthouse. The present light has an intensity of 45,000 candelas from a 100 watt twin filament bulb, and a range of 20 nautical miles. It was automated in 1994, and is now controlled by Trinity House from its centre at Harwich in Essex.

Strolling through a quiet floral lane

Point Robert Lighthouse

The Avenue

Maseline Harbour

Back on our Around Island Route, walk on and, rather than following the track as it goes right, walk straight on down a slightly narrower track with a dry stone wall on the left. Take the next left and carry on until reaching a metal gate on the left. Go through the gate, and follow the sign that says Footpath to Harbours. Walk on with the hedge on your right; the path can be seen in the far right-hand corner of the field.

We descend in a tunnel of vegetation. Go through a gate and when we emerge again we see the Maseline Harbour below us on the left. Follow the well-used path that curves around the harbour basin.

After descending some steps the starting point of our walk can be seen below. One final short ascent and we arrive on the road that leads up from the harbour. Turn left and in a few strides we are back where we started.

Sark: Maseline Harbour

Toilets: Yes

Food: Café

HERM,
AROUND ISLAND WALK

Distance: 4 Miles

Section 5 - **HERM**

Despite being the smallest island on the Channel Island Way, Herm has a charm all of its own, and an ambiance that lures people back time after time. Don't think that the short four mile route around the island is the only reason to visit, because even after an hour or so, it is hard to leave the tranquility of this little corner of the Channel Islands.

Some useful phone numbers

The dialling code for Herm is 01481.

Herm Administration Office: 750000

In an emergency dial 112 or 999

Suggested stops

Belvoir Bay Café

Between Belvoir Bay and Shell Beach – Public Toilets

Shell Beach Café

Herm Harbour – Public Toilets, Café, Restaurant, Pub

Herm Harbour

Toilets: Yes

Food: Cafe, Restaurant, Pub

Starting at Herm Harbour

This is another walk which starts almost the moment we set foot on dry land. Once disembarked at Herm Harbour, follow the pier inland towards the triangle of grass ahead, and at the fork in the track bear right. Pass a track on the right and a short path on the left that goes to the building with the beehive-shaped roof. This was the island prison during the boom years of the quarrying industry when 200 men were living and working on Herm.

The islands over to the right are Jethou and Crevichon, both bear clear signs of quarrying. Here the path forks – keep right to continue beside the sea.

Before the track begins to descend to Rosaire Steps, the low water landing place, go left and climb the granite steps, following the sign: To the South Coast cliff paths.

Starting at Rosaire Steps

If you disembark at Rosaire Steps, walk through the impressive crenellated granite entrance to the island, created by Prince Gebhard Blucher who was the island's tenant between 1889 and 1915, climb the track and take the granite steps on the right.

Jethou

The larger of the two islands off Herm's south-western coastline, Jethou has its own colourful history. Until the tenancy of Lt Colonel Montague Joseph Feilden, it was possible to hold the lease on both Herm and Jethou. Lt Colonel Feilden was the tenant from 1867 to 1877, and he spent thousands of pounds improving the island. He was the first tenant to develop the island for tourism: he opened a hotel, built Belvoir House, and established the oyster beds at Oyster Point.

However, the source of his income was questionable, especially as he had a

Passing Jethou on the way to Herm

motley crew of Bretons and Welshmen living on Jethou, firing at any fishermen who came too close. The reason they were so unfriendly soon became apparent, when customs officials found four bales of tobacco weighing 200 lbs hidden on Jethou. A year or so later, 50 barrels of brandy were found in the beach house on Jethou, and a further 27 were discovered on one of Feilden's four boats moored between Herm and Jethou. He was found guilty of smuggling brandy between France and Dorset and, some months later, decided to sell the remainder of his lease. Following Feilden's escapades, the Guernsey government felt it unwise to lease the islands to the same person. This clause was enforced until Sir Compton Mackenzie, the famous author and tenant of Herm, moved from Herm to Jethou in 1923.

Today, Jethou is leased from the States of Guernsey by philanthropist and keen yachtsman Sir Peter Ogden. Unlike Herm, the island is not open to the public and is still owned by the Crown.

Climb the steps, and before long we are on a level path with views over to the islands on the right. The path rises slightly, and, as we turn the south-west corner at Point Sauzebourge, a seascape of Sark and Brecqhou appears on the horizon.

The path descends and climbs; out to sea the tiny islands are home to flocks of sea birds. After a climb, we arrive at a T junction – here turn right and stay on the coastal path. At intervals beside the path are granite slabs – their resemblance to benches is not a coincidence, they are there as resting places for the weary.

The path diverts left around a deep fissure in the cliff side. Although the path goes very close, we are protected by a wooden barrier. This spot is known as Barbara's Leap. Surprisingly enough, Barbara is still remembered by people today as she 'leapt' in the early 1960s.

1. Barbara's Leap

Barbara Ward was the 19-year-old niece of Herm's gardener, John Pilorget, and she lived with her aunt and uncle at Fisherman's Cottage on Herm's west coast. One wet afternoon at the end of January 1961 she set off for a walk around the coast, and when she didn't return by nightfall the alarm was raised.

The search began at about 6pm, but two hours had passed before her cries for help were heard. When she was eventually found, she was trapped on a ledge about halfway down the 200ft cliff face. The St John Ambulance Brigade was called, and put to sea in the marine ambulance Flying Christine at around 8.45pm. The rescue was particularly hazardous, not only because of darkness, but because of over-hanging rocks and loose soil caused by heavy winter rain. The first person to reach her was St John Ambulance Brigade Area Commissioner Reginald Blanchford who, assisted by Private Brian Taylor, was able to administer pain-killing drugs, put her on a special stretcher and lower her down to the beach. She was then taken by dinghy to the Flying Christine. On arrival at St Peter Port Harbour in the early hours of the morning, she was taken by ambulance to the Princess Elizabeth Hospital. Despite her 80ft fall, Miss Ward was lucky enough to have only sustained heavy bruising and shock. After treatment Barbara returned to live on Herm and went on to marry the engineer of one of the Herm boats.

The bravery shown by Barbara's two rescuers, St John Ambulance Brigade Area Commissioner Reginald Blanchford and Private Brian Taylor, was recognised by the Queen in June 1961. Reginald Blanchford was made an Officer of the Order of the British Empire and Private Taylor was awarded the British Empire Medal.

Pheasants cross the path at regular intervals, seemingly oblivious of our presence. These were reintroduced recently, and are not the progeny of those introduced by Prince Blucher, who also imported roe deer, emus and wallabies during his tenure of Herm. The path winds through fir trees and climbs again to another junction; turn right here.

We descend for some distance. The large island on the right is Putrainez and the bay below is Puffin Bay. At the point, Cauchie de Robert, we get our first glimpse of Shell Beach away to the left. The sand looks so white that we could easily be in the Caribbean.

Leave the point and follow the path, it runs flat and level to Belvoir Bay, a sheltered sandy beach hidden below us only a few hundred yards away.

2. Belvoir Bay Café

Cross the concrete slipway to the bay, and proceed on to Shell Bay. Turning left, the track takes you across the island to the Manor Village and then to the Harbour. The path swings away to the left, and Shell Beach appears again before us.

We go through a pair of rusty gate posts, these were gates built to contain cattle that were overwintered on the common in the 1970s. We will see similar gate posts as we near the harbour on the western side of Herm. The path descends to the right and carries on to Shell Beach.

3. Shell Beach Café

Here we need to walk across the common. Follow the sandy track to the left, then take the first path across the grass on the right. With the sea on your right, continue along this route, although it may be rather faint in places. In due course, a clear wide track appears ahead in the grass – follow this and go over any crossroads that might intersect our route.

Toilets: Between Belvoir Bay and Shell Beach

Food: Café

Heading for Shell Beach

Shell Beach

The ground between us and the beach is heavily carpeted with sea holly. Carry on in the direction of the dunes ahead. Once the track reaches the tall marram grass it is easier to follow.

Out to sea is a collection of islands called The Humps. They are little self-contained islands; at low tide, each seems to have its own tiny sandy beach. The path rises as we approach the north-east corner at Alderney Point, and Mouisonniere Beach appears below us, with the east coast of Guernsey in the distance on the left. Brehon Tower is the Napoleonic defence that lies out to sea between Guernsey and Herm. It was built from Herm granite by Thomas Charles Du Putron between 1854 and 1856.

WARNING – Keep away from the beach-side edge of the dunes in case of collapse.

Follow the path as it bears left, descends and heads inland. Turn right at the T junction in the path, and pass the Obelisk.

4. The Obelisk

In their quest for big pieces of stone, Herm's quarrymen were not above destroying Neolithic monuments or burial sites. Because these large stones lay on the surface, they were a quick and easy option. They only needed cutting and they were ready for use.

In the late 1820s, the architect Benjamin Wyatt had designed the Duke of York's

Guernsey Calves in Herm

column and he especially wanted a piece of Herm granite for its base. This led the quarrymen to go to the monolith called Pierre aux Rats, at the northern end of the Common, which they then demolished for its stone.

When local fishermen discovered the loss of this vital day-mark, they demanded that something replace it, and the States of Guernsey ordered the Herm Granite Company to erect the obelisk. Sadly the stone pillaged from this site was not used on the column.

When the path emerges in an open area, with a number of random stones on the left, follow the path on the right beside the marram grass. Take the path on the extreme left that climbs, avoiding three paths that go off to the right.

Continue with the beach on your right. At the next point, Oyster Point, the shallow pool that we see at low tide is the remains of the oyster fishing that was established when Lt Colonel Montague Joseph Feilden was the tenant in the late 1860s.

Today, oysters are farmed on Herm's west coast, off Fisherman's Beach and Bear's Beach, and over a million oysters are grown here each year.

The hillock to the left is Le Petit Monceau. Here the path becomes clearer and sandier – go straight on at a crossroads and climb gently. As we climb, the Harbour and The White House come into view on the right. Avoid a path that goes off to the left, but proceed on.

When we emerge in an open area, follow the path as it curves right. Over to the left, we can see the sign post at Robert's Cross, this marks the start of the spine road that goes through the middle of the island. Bear right, avoiding a right that goes to The Bear's Beach, and climb gently to go between a lichen–covered wall and similar gate posts to those we saw near Belvoir Bay. At the sign post, follow the directions to Harbour Village and Rosaire Steps.

5. The Cemetery

A quick glance at the headstone would give the passer-by the impression that KW Conden was just an infant of two when he died, but a photograph of the cemetery taken in the 1880s shows that he was actually 22 years old. The photograph shows the month as April, but the year is hard to make out.

The popular belief is that the two people buried here died of cholera on their way from Jersey to England. As the ship's captain was not allowed to unload the corpses on Guernsey, he landed on Herm and they were buried here.

This is rather unlikely as it was the at the height of the quarrying industry on the island and Herm would have had a large population, who would not have wanted to bury the bodies.

The most plausible story is that these are the graves of two men who drowned when one of Lt Colonel Feilden's ships, The Ranger, sank off the island in 1873.

Once past the cemetery, walk straight on passing a left turn. The path is broad and well trodden with a dry stone wall on the left. Over to the left on the hill, we can see the various buildings of the Manor Village. In a few yards we pass a clearing with a white column in it. This is a 'leading mark' to help sailors navigate into Herm's harbour. When this column is aligned with another one further up the hillside, mariners know they are on a safe course into Herm's harbour.

Once past the shops and restaurants, bear right towards the Harbour, or carry on to Rosaire Steps.

Sunset from Fisherman's Beach over Guernsey